"Top producers don't wing it—they prepare. *Busin[...]* *[...] cess* shows you how to tie your message to the business outcomes executives actually care about. If you want to build more pipeline and close more deals, this book gives you the edge." —**Jeb Blount**, CEO of Sales Gravy and author of *Sales EQ*

"Want to quickly capture—and keep—a business leader's attention? If so, this book provides a clear and practical framework for engaging executives in a way that builds trust and accelerates decision-making. Well worth a read!" —**Jill Konrath**, bestselling author of *Selling to Big Companies* and *SNAP Selling*

"Trust is built when salespeople align what they offer with the real business challenges of their clients. In a world flooded with superficial pitches, *Business Acumen for Sales Success* fills a glaring gap by arming sellers with the clarity, discipline, and insight to speak in the language executives respect. This is more than a sales book—it's a bridge to credibility, value, and enduring trust." —**Stephen M.R. Covey**, bestselling author of *The Speed of Trust* and *Trust & Inspire*

"Salespeople who create value win. The ability to tie your solution to real business drivers isn't optional—it's a discipline. *Business Acumen for Sales Success* gives you the framework to move beyond product pitches and become the trusted advisor your clients actually need." —**Anthony Iannarino**, author of *The Only Sales Guide You'll Ever Need* and *The Lost Art of Closing*

"One of the most common criticisms revenue leaders have about their salespeople is that they lack the business acumen to effectively engage customers. Without a solid grasp of the dynamics of a customer's business, sellers will always struggle to draw them into the sales process, keep the relationship at a senior level, and successfully navigate tough negotiations. If any of this sounds familiar, the very first thing you should do is have your team read this book cover to cover. It's the best book on business acumen for sellers I've ever read." —**Matt Dixon,** coauthor of *The Challenger Sale, The JOLT Effect,* and *The Activator Advantage*

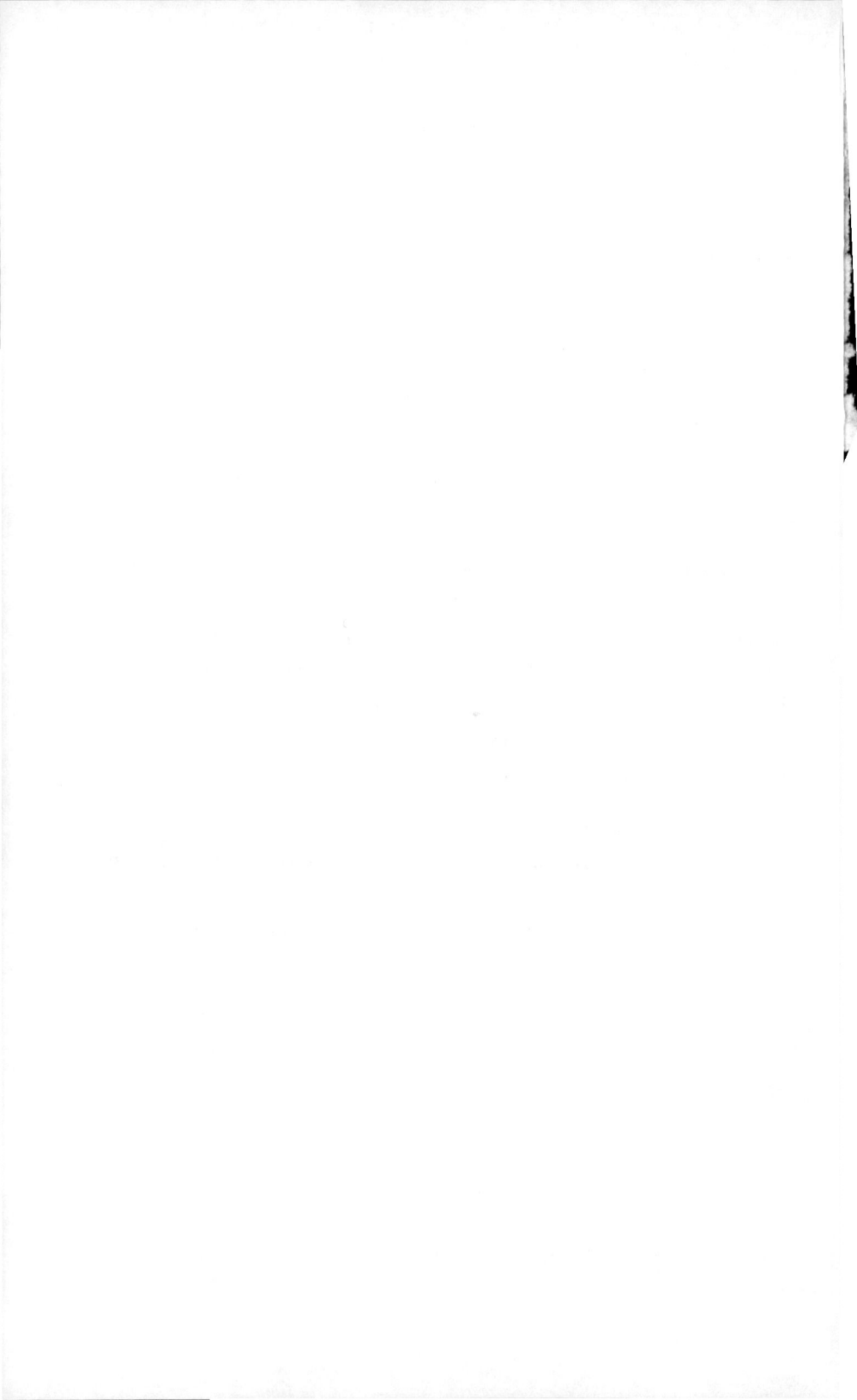

BUSINESS ACUMEN

for

SALES SUCCESS

-->

SELLING *the* BIG PICTURE
to BUILD TRUST *and* CLOSE MORE DEALS

KEVIN COPE

#1 *WSJ* and *NYT* Bestselling Author

BEN COOK

acumen*learning*

Published by Acumen Learning
Orem, Utah
www.AcumenLearning.com

Distributed by Acumen Learning LLC.

For ordering information or special discounts for bulk purchases, please contact Acumen Learning LLC at info@acumenlearning.com or 801-224-5444.

Cover design by Sheila Parr
Book design and composition by Draft Lab LLC

The 5 Business Drivers® is a registered trademark of Acumen Learning LLC.

Paperback ISBN: 979-8-9927482-1-5
Ebook ISBN: 979-8-9927482-2-2

First edition

BUSINESS ACUMEN

for

SALES SUCCESS

HOW TO USE THIS BOOK

WE'VE DESIGNED THIS BOOK TO BE A fast read with lots of easily accessible resources. The table of contents lists each major chapter section so that you can find what you need quickly. If you're prepping for your next sales call and need some quick insights into any of the 5 Drivers of your customer's business, turn to the "In Review" sections at the end of the chapters. If you just got an email from a client asking if you can help solve a business challenge, turn to the "Leverage" sections or the relevant section of the People chapter.

And if you want to level up your business acumen so that **you can become a stronger businessperson and a top sales performer**, read the book straight through. It will only take a few hours!

CONTENTS

CHAPTER 1

TOP SALESPEOPLE KNOW WHAT DRIVES THEIR CUSTOMER'S BUSINESS

YOU'VE JUST LEFT A MEETING WITH MICHELLE, and the sinking feeling in your gut is telling you you're not going to close this deal.

Michelle is a department head with one of your clients. She's the primary buyer for new project management software, and you're confident that your company has the ideal product. All of the research suggests that your offering stacks up well against the competition, especially for this kind of company.

But from the start of the meeting, which took you more than a month to book, Michelle seemed preoccupied and impatient. You decided the best course was to dive right into key features of your product, to engage her. Instead, she leaned back a bit more in her chair. You switched tactics and asked which of the features would be most important to her. She responded without much enthusiasm but shared that a few of the features you mentioned would be important to the teams using the software—so you launched into more detail about them. It didn't seem to help. She checked her phone twice.

You paused and shifted directions. "As you consider this new upgrade, what do you need to know to make the best decision possible?" To this question, she perked up a bit—but also delivered a confidence-busting statement. "You may have read about our earnings release this week. We missed our projections. Our CEO has promised investors that we'll improve our operating margin substantially over the next four quarters. Every department, including mine, has been asked to help make that happen. If we're going to invest in new software, we have to be able to show how it will improve the operating margin."

You started to panic inside but tried to keep your expression neutral. You kicked yourself for not knowing about the earnings release or what it might mean for the company—and especially this meeting. Then a flood of questions went through your mind: *What exactly is operating margin, and how exactly do you improve it?* Without knowing that, you really can't explain how your software will help.

You wrapped up the meeting by telling her that you were certain you would be able to help her achieve her goals and you would follow up with more information about how. But the truth is that you don't know the answers—and it likely showed.

> > >

Have you ever found yourself in this kind of situation? The data says that you probably have. We led with this example because it's so typical of how most salespeople engage with customers, leading with their products and pitch and missing the biggest opportunity—to connect with the customers' business strategies and challenges. Here's a hard truth for most salespeople: Your customers don't care much about your products or services. What they care about is how you can help them solve their very real business challenges.

Yet according to the research, only 20% of salespeople successfully reach executives' expectations and create value.[1] Those executives feel that 57% of the salespeople who contact them don't understand their industry, 75% don't understand their business, and 77% don't know how to help them tackle key issues. And like the hypothetical "you" in the story above, 70% aren't prepared for the questions these buyers ask. None of that helps a salesperson build essential trust with buyers, who are "more likely to consider a brand when a sales rep 'Demonstrates a clear understanding of our business needs and has a clear understanding of my role in the decision-making process.'"[2]

The good news in these dismal numbers? It's easy to set yourself apart from the crowd and stand out as a partner who brings insight and value to the table. When you showcase your understanding of their business, especially its current strategies and hurdles to growth— you build their confidence and your own credibility. And what we've proven in our work with hundreds of companies, including 35 of the Fortune 50, which represent some of the most sophisticated sales organizations in the world, is that all it takes is a few hours of education and then 15 minutes of focused prep for your next meeting. This book will help you do just that.

We'll help you build your business acumen, making you a more adept businessperson, advisor, and partner. Business acumen is powerful, sharp, street-smart insight into how any business operates, makes and spends money, becomes profitable, and sustains its growth now and into the future. We'll help you see the big picture of how a company uses its resources to achieve its goals, what buyers think about when making *business* decisions, and how to leverage that knowledge to close more sales. What we're offering is an MBA in six brief chapters and tools for assessing and connecting with everything your customers care about, every issue they deal with, and everything they factor into their decision to buy from you.

LEADERS, PROSPECTS, AND SALES METHODOLOGIES ASSUME YOU ALREADY KNOW THIS

While business acumen won't automatically make you a great salesperson, it's hard to become one without it, especially when selling to senior-level leaders or in complex sales situations.

Leaders, especially at the senior level, are searching for solutions to their broader challenges. To differentiate yourself and your products, you need to go beyond the obvious—the specifics of your offering and how it fits the client's stated needs—to understand and communicate how you can help your client *improve their business results*. And it doesn't take an MBA or an accounting degree to build the business acumen that will make you successful. **We've helped hundreds of thousands of people improve their business and financial acumen** so that they can better communicate with leaders, better lead their teams, prove the value of the work they do and recommendations they make—and advance their careers.

Every business needs better, more informed *businesspeople*, including on the sales team. Top sales performers have more than a good understanding of their offerings or great communication and negotiation skills. They have a deep grounding in business acumen that helps them add value for their clients but especially their own organizations. They increase the return on the investment their companies have made in developing the right products and services, marketing those services, and training their sales teams. And when you add that kind of value, your career takes off.

How does business acumen make the difference? We know that top sales performers have much more engaging conversations, ask far more questions *of* their prospects, and field far more questions *from* their prospects.[3] It's easier to do that when you aren't afraid of questions because you feel confident you'll know how to react and respond. The best of the best also spend 40% to 50% less time talking about product features. Instead, they're talking about the bigger picture and important business opportunities. By diving in and getting comfortable with the knowledge we'll share, you'll be able to do the same.

Now, this book doesn't replace the important sales skills you've learned, but it can dramatically increase your ability to master and leverage those skills. Most sales methodologies, like the Challenger Sale, SPIN selling, SNAP selling, and others, assume that you understand the money-making model of your customers, so they move right past it. Without that core knowledge, it's harder to apply those models successfully. With strong business acumen,

- You **close more deals** by being aligned with your client's financial objectives.

- You ask more effective questions that **build your credibility** and move conversations along faster.

- You **shorten the sales cycle** and get to decisions and results with your prospects faster.

- You **increase deal size** because you address bigger organizational challenges and company-wide strategies.

- You **build deeper relationships** because you offer value to specific people in specific roles and functions by connecting with their unique points of focus.

- You **negotiate more successfully** because you'll have a better understanding of the full value of your offerings to your client's business.

You might even find yourself more knowledgeable than the person on the other side of the table. You'll become a source of know-how and insight, a partner who helps them do *their* job better. And you won't have to ask a question like "What keeps you up at night?" because you'll go in having a good sense of the answer and how to help.

THIS BOOK IS DESIGNED TO DELIVER IMPORTANT KNOWLEDGE FAST—SO YOU CAN MAKE YOUR NEXT MEETING A SUCCESS

We get that as a salesperson, you're busy, and you need to learn what's important as fast as possible, right? We've organized this book so that you can read it from cover to cover or go to the specific information or resources that are most relevant to your immediate needs or situation. Every chapter also includes a quick summary of key points. Most importantly, we've kept it as short as possible!

Side note: We've kept the content on understanding financial statements to the essentials. If you need a deeper education in financial statements, because of your industry or clients, you can turn to our *New York Times* bestselling book, *Seeing the Big Picture*, which goes into more depth.

Part 1, The 5 Drivers of Every Business will provide you with a model or mental framework of how companies make and use money and what leaders think about, or *should* think about, as they make decisions.

You will learn about:

- The 5 Business Drivers—cash, profit, assets, growth, and people—and how they influence your customers' business decisions and strategies

- The most important metrics for those drivers—especially the ones most important to executive decision makers—and where to quickly find the information you need

- What the measures can reveal about a company so that you can deepen your understanding of your client's unique challenges and opportunities

- How to leverage the drivers in the sales process by aligning your solutions to them

- How to read the three core financial statements—the income statement, balance sheet, and statement of cash flows—so that you can gather vital information fast

Even if your client doesn't share the details of the company's financial performance publicly—maybe they're privately owned and aren't very transparent—they're thinking about, acting upon, and making decisions influenced by these drivers all the time. Understanding them helps you align with customers' challenges and opportunities throughout your sales process. And you can always turn to other companies in their industry that *are* public to discover what those challenges and opportunities might be.

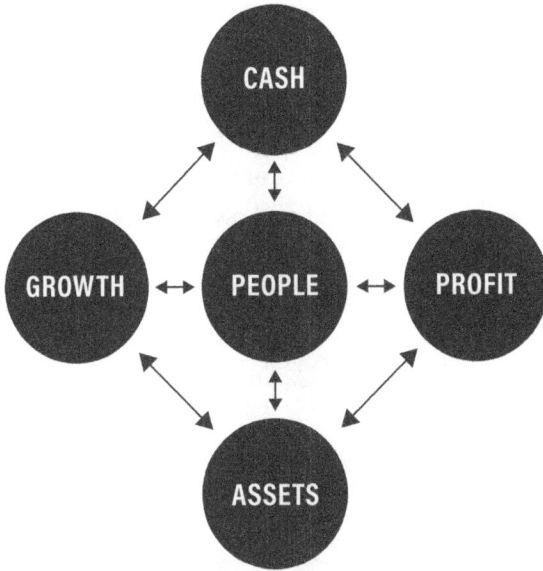

In **Part 2, Resources for Success in Your Next Sales Conversation**, we'll get even more practical. We'll give you:

- A simple three-step tool for assessing strategic focus, navigating the financials, and developing targeted value propositions that are aligned with your customer's challenges and objectives. You can use it to quickly gather and analyze information about the 5 Drivers and connect them to your solutions

- An explanation of how the function of the person you're talking to—from finance to R&D to customer service—influences what drivers they care about, and consequently your sales approach

- A one-page breakdown of the 5 Drivers in 25 key industries, creating a quick reference guide you can come back to again and again to understand how your client stacks up—where they're strong and where they might need help

With these accessible and highly practical tools and models, you'll be more prepared than 75% of your competitors for your next meeting.

You can also go to our website, SellingtheBigPicture.com, for even more resources, including downloadable versions of the tools we're offering, videos that take the ideas deeper, and more.

Our goal is to help you better connect with your clients' businesses and position yourself as a resource for adding real, lasting value to their organizations. We can't wait to hear how you apply what you learn and what you accomplish.

PART 1

THE 5 DRIVERS OF EVERY BUSINESS

$

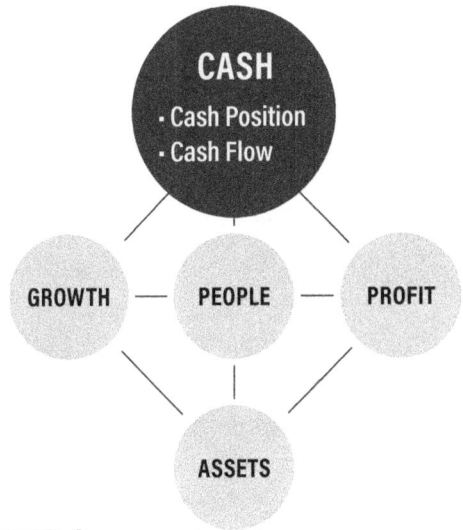

CHAPTER 2

CASH

"I like to carry some cash because you feel like you can
cope with any situation—such as being mugged."[4]
—Comedian and actor David Mitchell

SHAY WORKED FOR A COMPANY THAT MADE factory equip-
ment. They had launched a new product line, and all of her research
and homework suggested it was ideal for one of her customers. But
when she approached her contact, she got a quick no: "There's no money in our budget for new equipment this year." Shay's leaders had given
her the leeway to offer solid discounts if necessary, but for this client,
that didn't matter. They were investing their cash in other things.

Shay went to her sales manager and proposed a solution: Could
she offer 0% financing instead of the discount? Shay's company didn't
always offer customer financing, but they *could*. They had enough cash
reserves to take a small risk. And Shay knew that even though her client
might not have the cash to cover the full cost now, they were a successful
business with strong sales every month. They had enough cash coming
in to absorb the monthly payment.

Shay laid out the plan for her contact, who was tentatively optimistic. A week later the purchase had been approved and the paperwork was underway. The deal was a win for everybody because Shay leveraged her business acumen, especially understanding how her customer earned and used its cash.

Cash is the first of the 5 Business Drivers because **it's the fuel that propels a business—every business**, from giants like Walmart and Apple to the small neighborhood flower shops or mom-and-pop diners, and for every one of your clients or customers. Cash is the enabler of every strategy and possibly the best indicator of whether a company is going to be around next quarter or next year. As Warren Buffett wrote, cash "is to a business as oxygen is to an individual."[5] And as we tell the sales professionals in our courses, if your customer is flush with cash, they'll buy from you without a lot of worry. And if they're short of cash, it's the only thing they'll be thinking about.

In this chapter, we'll help you understand *why* cash is important to your customers, *how* they generate it and measure it, and what *you* can do to align your value proposition with it or show how your offerings can positively impact it. Can you imagine how valuable those insights might be in your next sales conversation? Let's dive in.

CASH TELLS YOU WHETHER A COMPANY CAN SURVIVE AND THRIVE

Lack of cash is one of the primary reasons companies fail. Without it, a business can't pay its bills, can't pay its employees, can't buy the goods it needs to produce the products or services it sells, and can't generate revenue or profit. Eventually that company will go out of business.

On the flip side, with a reasonable amount of cash on hand or the ability to easily get more—by earning it or borrowing it, for example—a company can weather tough market and economic storms, can grow by investing in new software or research or equipment, and can take advantage of new market opportunities, even buying out competitors.

Simply put: a business must have cash to survive and thrive.

You probably don't need much proof of that statement, but you can find it everywhere. You can look at the number of companies that went out of business during the COVID-19 pandemic because they didn't have the cash to survive the shutdowns or the fall-off in business. Estimates put the number of restaurant closures alone at 70,000 to 90,000. It's why the federal government stepped in to offer paycheck protection loans (that were forgiven) to small and medium-sized businesses—giving them cash they could use to pay employees and keep their doors open.

You can go further back to 2008, when major financial institutions, such as Bear Stearns, Lehman Brothers, Fannie Mae, and Freddie Mac and at least 22 major banks, either went bankrupt or were purchased at rock-bottom prices because they didn't have enough cash and couldn't get more of it.

And if you're old enough to remember getting the Sears Christmas catalog every year, you probably felt sad when that 130-year-old company that had once been the largest retailer in the world—their innovative catalog model was the precursor to online shopping—went bankrupt in 2019 because it wasn't bringing in enough cash to survive.

No matter how long a company has been in business, how famous it is, or how big it has become, it can't ignore the importance of cash. **Most leaders know cash is the lifeblood of their company, so every CEO, COO, entrepreneur, or investor is laser-focused on trying to generate it.**

A little information about your customer's cash *position* and cash *flow*, whether it's a public company or private, can tell you a lot about how strong that company is in the short term and give you clues about how well it'll do in the long term.

Cash Position

To understand the full picture of a company's cash strengths or weaknesses, and to spot opportunities to align your sales approach with them, you have to look at both the cash position and the cash flow. Together, they tell a more complete story.

Usually, when businesspeople use the term *cash*, they're referring to a company's cash *position*—how much cash a company has at a specific point in time. It's the cash that has come in that hasn't gone out, or been spent, yet. It's like the money sitting in your savings account. Public companies report this at the end of every quarter and at the close of the fiscal year.

Having cash on hand to use if the going gets rough is a good thing. After the Great Recession of 2008, a lot of companies began to save more cash to protect themselves from future economic downturns, and that might have helped during the COVID-19 pandemic.

When it comes to cash position, there is no rule of thumb about how much cash a company should keep on hand. The average ratio of cash to sales or revenue across the companies in the S&P 500 is around 25%, but every company differs in how much cash or reserves it needs for operations and to protect itself in case of a sudden financial hit. Beyond that, cash can be reinvested to keep the company growing. Apple, for example, is holding onto a lot more cash than it needs to run the business. Why? Beyond the basics of protecting itself, the cash provides "dry powder" in case Apple finds a company it wants to acquire. For instance, Apple bought more than 30 AI technology companies, most of them relatively small, in 2023 alone. Second, leaders can invest it in R&D and equipment updates, even when the economy might be struggling. Third, they can move quickly and decisively if they want to create a new product line. Those are the benefits to any business that holds a good amount of cash.

CFOs, CEOs, and financial managers have to **balance the need to keep some cash tucked under the mattress, so to speak, the need to reinvest cash in the company to keep it growing (more on that in Chapter 5), and demands from shareholders for dividends and share buybacks.** When making decisions about cash, they consider factors like the seasonality of the company's sales, economic and market forecasts, plans and strategies that might require a big one-time investment, how easy it would be to borrow money or sell stock to raise cash, and more. If they hold on to too little, they're at risk if something about their business goes sideways. If they hold on to too much, they miss out on growth opportunities, or investors start wondering why the company isn't paying higher dividends to stockholders.

For example, more than a decade ago, Apple was sued by a prominent shareholder, Greenlight Capital, because it felt Apple was sitting on much more cash than it needed. The shareholder wanted Apple to return a portion of the extra cash back to shareholders through dividends and stock buybacks, which Apple began doing. While Apple executives enjoy a large cash reserve, they have to balance the benefits with the interests of shareholders.

Cash Flow

Cash *flow* refers to the amount of cash that flows through a business, or is generated by the business, over a certain period of time. It's like the money that flows in and out of your checking account. You can also think of cash flow as an equation:

$$\text{Cash in} - \text{Cash out} = \text{Cash flow}$$

On the surface, it can seem like cash flow and profit are the same thing, but they aren't. We'll explain the differences and why both numbers matter in the next chapter.

A company can have either a *positive cash flow*—total cash inflows are greater than total cash outflows—or a *negative cash flow*—outflows are greater than inflows. We're sure you probably guessed that a positive cash flow is better than a negative cash flow. Investors, shareholders, and employees should be concerned about a company that is *consistently* paying out more cash than it's bringing in, unless the company is new. Some start-ups take a while to generate a positive cash flow, relying on cash from investors or loans early on. But negative cash flow in a mature company is a red flag. If it's a temporary state of affairs and the company has a strong cash position, it's not a huge issue. But if cash flow from core business operations has been trending downward for a while and the company can't adjust its operations to bring in more cash over time, it will eventually run out of cash and be forced to declare bankruptcy.

Many investors, financial analysts, and company leaders consider cash flow, especially cash generated from the company's core business operations, to be the most important indicator of a company's financial health and ability to survive and make money over the long term. Some say that cash is king, but in assessing the future of a company, cash flow is king. Companies rich in cash or with a strong cash position can seem strong on paper, but a company's ability to generate cash in the future is often more important. And it's one of the most important measures or concepts to tie your solutions and value proposition to because you're proving how you can help the company succeed in the long term. We'll share the levers you can use to do that later in the chapter.

Even companies that don't seem to have a very strong cash position, in comparison to companies in other industries, for instance, but have a strong cash flow can be powerhouses. Walmart is a great example. Because it sells through such a high volume of its inventory every single day, it has great cash flow. But it has to invest its cash in inventory, warehouses, retail property, and more, so it doesn't always have a lot of cash on hand. We're talking in relative terms, obviously—Walmart had "just" $9 billion in cash and cash equivalents at the end of its 2025 fiscal year (ending January 31st, 2025), with revenue of $681 billion. That's a 1.3% cash-to-revenue ratio, compared to the average 25% that we mentioned earlier for the S&P 500.

The long game for any business is to spend less cash than it brings in, and that can make your job as a salesperson a bit harder! But when you understand where your customers' cash is coming from and how they spend it to earn *more*, your job gets easier.

How Companies Get and Use Cash

If you want a model for a company that excels at generating cash, just look at Apple. It generates so much cash, the company can't spend it fast enough. Let's use Apple to understand how companies get and use cash through three essential business activities.

Operating Activities   We've mentioned operations a few times, so let's clarify what we mean. Operating activities are all the core activities a company has to engage in to produce and sell its products or services, with the goal of making money. If you look at Apple's operating activities at a basic level, they're researching and designing new products, manufacturing them, marketing and selling them, collecting payment from the customers or retailers who order them, and then shipping them out. Cash comes in from sales generated from those operations, and cash goes out in the form of expenses for things the company requires to keep operating, like raw materials, employee salaries, and so on.

As a salesperson, you're tied into operating activities. You generate revenue (cash in) for your own company through sales. For your customers, you represent cash out. If they're going to pay for your products or services, which they likely use in their own operating activities, they will want to ensure the investment allows them to generate or save more cash than they've spent.

Operating activities are the most important and best source of cash because the company earned it. If a company has a strong positive number for the cash generated from operating activities, it's more likely that it will be able to weather fluctuations in the market. And if you want to increase your chances of closing a sale, show how your product or service can improve your client's cash generated from operating activities.

Investing Activities   When engaging in investing activities, companies use cash to purchase assets, like equipment or facilities, real estate, stocks or bonds (marketable securities), and even other companies. Investing activities also enable companies to generate cash by earning interest or dividends on their investments and selling investments for more money than they paid. For instance, Apple has purchased at least 100 companies since it was founded. Companies use cash in this way because they believe they'll be able to use the assets they invest in to generate more cash as part of their operating activities—and because they understand that they must consistently reinvest in themselves in order to support innovation and growth.

Investing activities come with a bit of risk because a return on the investment (cash in greater than cash out) is not a guarantee. If a company needed cash, it could sell an asset that it invested in, but then it wouldn't have the asset to use anymore or it might have to sell the asset at a loss if it needs cash fast. A carpenter wouldn't sell his tools for cash, right? Because he wouldn't be able to generate more cash in the long run. And a real estate investor wouldn't sell a building when the market was down unless they had no choice.

Financing Activities   Finally, a company can get cash by borrowing it from banks or other financial institutions or by selling shares of company stock to investors. And if you were savvy enough to purchase Apple stock when it was first issued in 1980, congratulations! A company also uses cash in financing activities to pay dividends to stockholders, buy back shares of stock, or pay down its debt. The hope with financing activities is that the company can use the money it takes in to *generate more money from operations.*

You may not have a lot of direct influence on your clients' financing activities, but if they have to finance their purchase with you, the more you understand about how financing activities impact cash flow the better prepared you'll be. Remember Shay from the beginning of the chapter? A financing option—a zero-cost financing option—made the difference in her ability to close the deal. Of course, that rarely happens. Usually financing comes with a cost. If market interest rates are high or your customer has a shaky credit rating or a low stock price, the cost of financing will be higher and will eat into their cash flow and other financial measures.

> > >

Again, cash generated from the core business (operating activities) is the best source of cash because a company has earned it. Raising cash by selling assets (investing activities) is a one-time event, because at the end, the asset is gone. Borrowing money (financing activities) can be an ongoing activity, but the company has to pay that money back—with interest. It's tempting, and sometimes necessary, for leaders to take risks when they need cash *now*, but the best way to generate cash is to earn it.

TWO VITAL CASH MEASURES

To help you understand how strong your clients are—and how you might bring value to them—let's look at the two most common and important cash measures you'll hear leaders talk about or see in financial reports. Even if you can't access financial statements, understanding what these measures mean will help you speak the language of executives.

Cash and Cash Equivalents—Cash Position

Cash and cash equivalents is the cash that can be *used now*. At the end of Apple's 2024 fiscal year, they were holding onto about $65 billion—with a *b*—in cash and cash equivalents. But how is that number calculated? Is it just a lump sum sitting in a bank account somewhere? Not quite.

- *Cash* includes currency, coin, and even checks in hand but not yet deposited. It also includes cash balances in accounts of all types at banks and other financial institutions.

- *Cash equivalents* are any short-term securities or other financial instruments, such as stock market or money market investments, certificates of deposit, or short-term treasury bills, that can be sold or converted to cash quickly, without much risk of loss, usually within 90 days.

You can't pay bills with money you don't have yet, so a company's cash and cash equivalents do not include some financial line items that might be included in other measures, such as accounts receivable or inventory.

A quick note: In the news, you might hear that Apple is holding onto about $150 billion in cash, a number much, much larger than the official cash on hand and cash equivalents. That's because they're including other kinds of assets that are not considered cash but could be turned into cash fairly easily if necessary. Essentially, Apple is generating so much cash that they have to put it somewhere, and they put it into the stock market or other investments, just like any of us might in order to get a better return than if that cash was sitting in a savings account. The value of those investments shows up on the balance sheet, not the statement of cash flows. In 2024, for example, Apple was holding onto *$126 billion* in marketable securities, above and beyond their actual cash position.

Cash Generated from Operating Activities— Cash Flow

As we've said, cash generated from a company's core operations is one of the best measures of its long-term health, so it's one of the two vital cash measures every businessperson should understand. Like the simple equation we shared before, cash generated from operating activities is cash that flows in from sales minus cash that flows out or that the company spends to keep its core operations functioning. This is why it's often called *net cash generated from operating activities* on financial statements.

At the end of this chapter, we'll show you where to find these two critical cash measures on the statement of cash flows.

LEVERAGING CASH IN THE SALES PROCESS

What cash can tell you, as a salesperson, is where your customers are headed, what strategies they're putting into place, and what the future might look like. For instance, in a recent quarterly earnings call, here's what Tim Cook said about Apple's cash position:

"Operating cash flow was strong at $22.7 billion ... We ended the quarter with $162 billion in cash and marketable securities."[6] *Translation:* We have so, so much cash. In just three months, we generated $22.7 billion from our core business operations, and now we're sitting on $162 billion.

"We repaid $3.2 billion in maturing debt and commercial paper was unchanged sequentially, leaving us with total debt of $105 billion." *Translation:* We're using that extra cash to pay down our debt.

"During the quarter, we returned over $27 billion to shareholders, including $3.7 billion in dividends and equivalents and $23.5 billion through open-market repurchases of $130 million Apple's shares. Given the continued confidence we have in our business now and into the future, our Board has authorized today an additional $110 billion for share repurchases." *Translation:* We're also using our cash to pay higher and higher dividends to stockholders and to buy back shares of our stock that are out in the market. We know all of this makes us more appealing to investors and drives our stock price up.

Frankly, if you're selling to Apple, all of this is good news. You don't have to worry that they're going to say no simply because they don't have the cash to complete a purchase with you.

Let's go back to Shay, from the beginning of the chapter, who was in a slightly different position. Shay understood that while her client's cash position might not support a purchase decision, their cash flow could if she could work it out. But that's not the whole story. Shay had to prove the value of the investment, or the benefit of committing to the new line of machinery. She leveraged two critical points of value: the machinery was more efficient than what they were currently using and it reduced errors. *Her client could improve the cash generated from operating activities* because they could produce more of their products faster and with less expense. And Shay knew that this was an important point to make because she had looked at the statement of cash flows and seen that while the net cash generated from operating activities was solid, it had also fallen every year for the past three years.

If she hadn't been able to make that argument, and likely back it up with data, the financing proposal might not have gone anywhere. So, the 10 minutes Shay spent downloading the report from the company's website and reviewing it gave her the basis for a strong, successful sales strategy.

She understood that regardless of the strength of a company's cash position or cash flow now, what leaders and investors really want is for the cash generated from operating activities to increase year over year. Which is why Tim Cook led with Apple's "strong" operating cash flow in his remarks. An upward trend means the core business is generating more cash as the company grows, operations are becoming more efficient, and leaders have a better understanding of what resources they need and when.

When you're thinking about how best to meet your customers where they are and help them achieve their goals, remember that *leaders will consistently take action to improve cash flow from operations.*

Consider these questions:

- Can you help them **collect money from customers faster** and more efficiently?

- Can you create opportunities to **reduce expenses**?

- Can you prove that investing in your product, even if they have to borrow money to do so, will help them provide more or better products and services—and **boost their ability to sell more**? This is what Shay did.

- Can you offer **better financing terms** to reduce the money they have to spend over the quarter or year?

- Can you help them **better utilize their inventory** to improve cash flow and reduce expenses?

If your offering can help your customer reduce expenses, make better use of its existing assets, get work done more efficiently, or improve sales of its products and services, say so! Your buyer will immediately perk up. Next, we'll help you understand the statement of cash flows, where you can gather financial insights. Even if your client isn't a publicly traded company, you can learn a lot about their perspective on cash by reviewing the statements of their closest publicly traded competitors or reading any big news about investments they've made, debts they've taken on, or struggles they're experiencing.

And remember, you can use the resources in Part 2 to help you capture what matters most about your clients' cash position and cash flow, understand what challenges they face or goals they've set, and align your sales approach with what you discover. You can also download the tools at SellingtheBigPicture.com.

A QUICK GUIDE TO
READING FINANCIAL STATEMENTS

Throughout this book, we'll help you pull important information from the three essential financial statements that reflect the 5 Drivers of any business:

» **The income statement**, which is often called a statement of earnings, a statement of operations, a profit and loss statement, or a P&L for short

» **The balance sheet**, occasionally called the statement of financial position, which shows assets, liabilities, and shareholder's equity

» **The statement of cash flows**, which shows how much cash a company has, where it comes from, and where it's going

As you begin to learn about these statements, starting with the statement of cash flows, here are a few things to consider.

» **You can find the financial statements for publicly traded companies on their website.** A quick search online will usually bring you right to them, or to the right page on their website, typically an investors page. Privately held companies may or may not share their financial statements online, and you may have to do a bit more sleuthing to learn about the drivers. More on how to do that in Part 2.

» **Statements don't always reflect current financial reality.** Most large organizations use an accounting approach called accrual-basis accounting. Revenue and expenses are "booked" or recorded in the accounting system when transactions take place, not necessarily when the money is actually received or spent. A business might close 100 sales in a month and show the revenue from those sales in some financial reports, but they don't necessarily have the cash from the customers yet.

» **The amounts on the financial statements of larger companies are often truncated.** At the top of the statements, you'll see the notation "In thousands," "000s dropped," "In millions," or "000,000s dropped." When you read the numbers, make sure you add those missing zeros: $470 becomes $470,000 if the statement is presented in thousands but $470,000,000 if the statement is presented in millions.

» **You need to read the line item labels carefully, not just the numbers themselves.** Is the number negative or positive? Subtracted from the total or added to it? You need to read the line item labels to really know. For example, on some reports, negative numbers are shown in parenthesis. However, items that are subtracted from the total are not usually presented as negatives. For example, on the income statement, the different kinds of expenses listed aren't shown as "negative" numbers, even though they are tallied and subtracted from revenue or sales numbers by the end of the statement.

» **Many reports and line items have more than one name and look different between industries and companies.** Even though the fundamental organization of financial statements is consistent, companies may label items differently (revenue might be called net sales, for instance), often based on what industry they're in. After reviewing a few, though, you'll be able to find and understand the most important items.

» **Numbers are only meaningful in context.** Other than the amount, we'll ask you to look at three basic characteristics of most metrics:

  - Trend: Is the value going up or down over time, and in the right direction? By what percentage is it moving up or down? Is the rate of change accelerating or slowing?

  - Ratio: Compare the item to other relevant items, like profit to revenue. Is the ratio in line with expectations, and how is it trending? We'll explore the most important ratios (like profit margin) for specific drivers.

  - Industry and competitor analysis: How do these numbers compare to the industry (you can find this information in Part 2) and key competitors?

» **Public companies follow special rules and regulations for reporting, with lots of acronyms.** The Securities and Exchange Commission (SEC) requires that the financial statements of all public companies be audited and prepared according to generally accepted accounting principles (GAAP), which are developed by the Financial Accounting Standards Board (FASB). The IRS uses the same rules to calculate a company's income taxes. Companies outside of the US often follow the international financial reporting standards (IFRS). If you often work with international corporations, go to our website (SellingtheBigPicture.com) for more information on reading IFRS-based statements. Throughout this book, we'll be using examples that follow the US's GAAP.

» **Most reports show more than one year or quarter.** One SEC and GAAP requirement is that financial statements show three years of data on the income statement and statement of cash flows and two on the balance sheet. This makes it easier to spot trends.

THE STATEMENT OF CASH FLOWS

The statement of cash flows, or cash flow statement, offers vital information for a salesperson: In a couple of minutes, it can tell you how well your customer's core business is doing, whether they've got the cash to make buying from you an easier or harder decision, and even what strategies they're using to succeed in the short and long term.

At its core, the statement shows the amount of cash a company takes in and uses during a particular reporting period, usually a quarter or a fiscal year. And it shows the cash generated from each of the three activities we described—operations, investments, and financing—and is built on this basic equation:

	Cash from (or used in) operating activities
+	Cash from (or - used in) investing activities
+	Cash from (or - used in) financing activities
=	Net increase or decrease in cash and cash equivalents

It's a lot like a well-organized bank statement for your checking and savings accounts. Positive numbers on the statement mean a *source of cash* or cash inflow for the business. Negative numbers, usually shown in parentheses on this report, mean *cash used* by or cash outflow for the business. In the example shown here, for Apple, we've highlighted the important numbers we described in the last section.

Apple's Consolidated Statement of Cash Flows
(in millions)

	Years Ended		
	Sept. 30, 2024	Sept. 30, 2023	Sept. 24, 2022
Operating activities:			
Net income	$ 93,736	$ 96,995	$ 99,803
Adjustments to reconcile net income to cash generated by operating activities:			
Depreciation and amortization	11,445	11,519	11,104
Share-based compensation expense	11,688	10,833	9,038
Deferred income tax expense/(benefit)			895
Other	(2,266)	(2,227)	111
Changes in operating assets and liabilities:			
Accounts receivable, net	(3,788)	(1,688)	(1,823)
Inventories	(1,046)	(1,618)	1,484
Vendor non-trade receivables	(1,356)	1,271	(7,520)
Other current and non-current assets	(11,731)	(5,684)	(6,499)
Accounts payable	6,020	(1,889)	9,448
Other current and non-current liabilities	15,552	3,031	6,110
Cash generated by operating activities	**118,254**	**110,543**	**122,151**
Investing activities:			
Purchases of marketable securities	(48,656)	(29,513)	(76,923)
Proceeds from maturities of marketable securities	51,211	39,686	29,917
Proceeds from sales of marketable securities	11,135	5,828	37,446
Payments for acquisition of property, plant, and equipment	(9,447)	(10,959)	(10,708)
Other	(1,308)	(1,337)	(2,086)
Cash used in investing activities	2,935	(3,705)	(22,354)
Financing activities:			
Payments for taxes related to net share settlement of equity awards	(5,441)	(5,431)	(6,223)
Payments for dividends and dividend equivalents	(15,234)	(15,025)	(14,841)
Repurchases of common stock	(94,949)	(77,550)	(89,402)
Proceeds from issuance of term debt, net	—	5,228	5,465
Repayments of term debt	(9,958)	(11,151)	(9,543)
Proceeds from/(Repayments of) commercial paper, net	3,960	(3,978)	3,955
Other	(361)	(581)	(160)
Cash used in financing activities	(121,983)	(108,488)	(110,749)
Increase/(Decrease) in cash, cash equivalents, and restricted cash	(794)	5,760	(10,952)
Cash, cash equivalents, and restricted cash, ending balances	**$ 29,943**	**$ 30,737**	**$ 24,977**

To get to net cash generated by operating activities, we start at the top of the statement with net income, often called profit and a number you'll see again in the next chapter. Then line item by line item, we make positive or negative adjustments to that number to determine *actual* cash received *from* operations minus *actual* cash spent *in* operations as of the date of the report. In the example, you can see at the top of the statement that Apple's net income is $93,736,000,000, or almost $94 billion. And you can see a series of line items that show positive or negative adjustments, which increase or decrease the *actual* cash flow or cash generated by that amount.

Apple generated more than $118 billion in cash from its operating activities. With that much cash generated, it can easily afford to invest in research and development, buy companies, pay dividends, buy back stock, and *still* keep a huge amount of cash on hand.

Cash and Cash Equivalents, or the company's cash position, at the end of the reporting period is shown at the bottom of the statement because all activities feed that number. And because the financial statements are linked to each other, you can also find it toward the top of the balance sheet, because cash is an asset. The current cash and cash equivalents is calculated by starting with the cash and cash equivalents at the end of the prior period, found at the bottom of the next column. For Apple, it's over $30 billion. Then you make adjustments, whether positive or negative, for the cash in and cash out from operations, investing, and financing during the period. Apple's activities resulted in a decrease in their cash and cash equivalents, or a drop in their cash position, over the year of $794 million, ending with cash and cash equivalents of almost $30 billion.

We mentioned earlier that some sources say Apple is holding on to more than $200 billion in cash. Remember that they're often adding in other assets that could be easily turned into cash, such as marketable securities.

With a quick glance at the bottom of the statement of cash flows, you can gather quite a lot of information. But be careful. While you don't have to understand every line item of every financial report, you should take a minute to scan them so that you better understand the totals. For instance, you might think that it's a bad sign that Apple's cash and cash equivalents dropped by almost $800 million from 2023 to 2024. But look at how much money they spent just to buy back their stock in the line item "Repurchases of common stock." Why would they spend almost $95 billion on that? Well, given that they had been sued by investors in the past, they're returning some of the money they earn to stockholders. But they're also reducing the number of stockholders they have, and they're potentially increasing the price of each share of the stock, due to the shares of stock on the market becoming more scarce. This makes it easier to raise money in the future.

So no, that drop in cash and cash equivalents wasn't a sign that Apple was in trouble. Not by a long shot.

If you need a more in-depth walkthrough of the statement of cash flows or any of the financial statements, you can pick up our book *Seeing the Big Picture*, which devotes much more time to reading and analyzing financial statements, or you can go to SellingtheBigPicture. com for other helpful resources.

> > >

No matter where you are in the sales cycle with a client, understanding their cash challenges and strategies and how you can align your offerings with them will improve your value proposition and your partnership. So take the time right now to assess your most important customer's cash position and cash flow and answer this basic question: How can you help?

> > > > > CASH IN REVIEW

» Cash is the fuel of every business. All companies require cash to operate, pay bills, and invest for the future. Lack of cash is a primary reason businesses fail.

» Cash *position* is the amount of cash on hand and in financial accounts, plus short-term securities or other items easily convertible to cash within 90 days *at a specific point in time*. A business with too much cash might be missing opportunities to invest in the company. And shareholders prefer that excess cash be invested or given back to them as dividends or by repurchasing their stock.

» Cash *flow* refers to the amount of cash that flows through a business or is generated by the business *over a certain period of time*, usually a quarter or a year. You can also think of cash flow as an equation: Cash in – Cash out = Cash flow. The ability to generate cash flow is usually considered more important than the cash position.

» A business gets and uses cash in three basic activities: (1) operations of core business; (2) investing, or buying and selling assets; and (3) financing, by receiving and paying back loans (debt), paying dividends, or buying back its own stock. The most important is cash generated from operations because it reflects money a company actually earned and is a major indicator of a company's long-term health.

» Two important measures are cash and cash equivalents and net cash generated by operating activities, the measure of cash flow from operations.

» As a salesperson, you have to consider that you represent a cash outflow for your customer. If you want to convince them to part with cash and invest it in your products or solutions, you'll need to show them how the investment can help them generate more cash or improve their cash flow from operations in the long run.

» You can find measures of the cash position and cash flow from operations on the statement of cash flows. It measures cash generated based on this basic equation:

Cash from (or used in) operating activities
+   Cash from (or – used in) investing activities
+   Cash from (or – used in) financing activities
_____
=   Net increase or decrease in cash and cash equivalents

» It begins with the cash and cash equivalents from the prior period, makes adjustments to calculate *actual* cash flow during the period from the three activities, and ends with the new, current total of cash and cash equivalents.

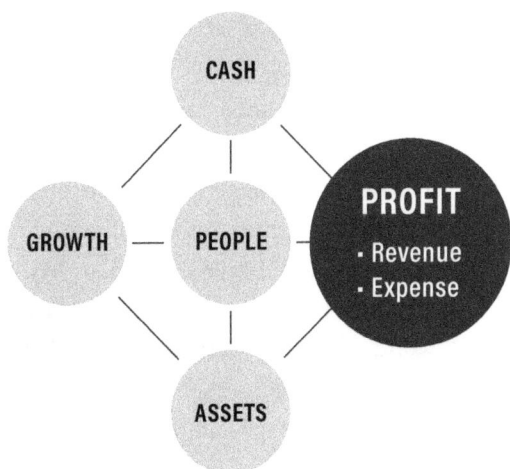

CHAPTER 3

PROFIT

"Profit is like oxygen, food, water, and blood for the body;
they are not the *point* of life,
but without them there is no life."[7] —Jim Collins

WE ONCE HAD A SALES REP IN our training program, we'll call
him Lucas, who was struggling to get clients to adopt his company's
newest shipping containers. They were more expensive, and for many of
his clients, the containers they were already using still had some years of
life left in them. The new containers maximized the freight that could
be carried in an innovative way, but when Lucas shared the increase in
cubic feet with customers, they weren't that impressed.

During the training, one idea stood out for Lucas: the expense associated with every shipment a company made in gasoline, in driver salaries, in tolls, in loading. The new containers were much more efficient,
and even though they came with a higher price tag, they would reduce
costs elsewhere.

He gathered shipping data from one of his clients, a pharmaceutical company, calculated how much more they could transport in a new

container, and then calculated how much they might save. With the new containers, they could decrease the number of deliveries by 16% and save an average of $750 with every container full of goods they shipped out. Even with the increased price and upfront expense, his customers could save more than they would spend over time, increasing their profit in the long term. They would also be able to tell the world what they were doing to reduce their greenhouse gas emissions and reduce the number of trucks on the country's highways, bolstering their brand image and potentially improving their sales.

Lucas made the sale and, because of his clear understanding of the financial pressure points for his customer, became a trusted advisor.

If cash is the fuel of a business, as we wrote in the last chapter, then profit determines how long the engine will keep running.

Also called net income, the bottom line, or earnings, profit is the difference between how much a company makes by selling goods and services, also called sales, revenues, or the top line, and how much it costs to produce and sell them, or its expenses.

Revenue – Expenses = Profit or net income

Obviously, companies want to sell their goods and services for more than they cost to create or provide! What you're selling represents an expense for your customers, so it's up to you to make a good business case that the expense is worth it. How will it help them increase their revenues or reduce other expenses so that their profits ultimately grow? Understanding how your clients calculate, think about, and communicate about profit will help you answer that question and spot your best sales opportunities.

PROFIT GIVES YOU IMPORTANT CLUES ABOUT A COMPANY'S STAYING POWER

In 2022, UPS hit two milestones: its annual *revenue* hit $100 billion for the first time since it was founded in 1907. And the company reported the highest profit ever earned from its core business—more than $13 billion. Given the rise in online shopping during the COVID pandemic, UPS was sure to see a boom in business.

If revenue increases dramatically, it's easier to increase your profit. That's pretty obvious. But while UPS's revenue grew by about 11%, its profit for 2022 grew by a full 20% because it also reduced expenses—the sign of a healthy growing company that's becoming more efficient over time. The results for 2023 and even 2024 tell a slightly different story, one we'll share later, which is why it's important to look at a few years of data to get the full picture.

A company's financial health and future is ultimately determined by how profitably it can conduct its *core business* over time—increasing sales, controlling expenses, earning more income, and generating more cash. For publicly held companies, Wall Street uses profitability to determine value, and stock price depends on what investors and analysts believe about a company's future profitability. Privately held companies are just as concerned with profit—maybe more so depending on the nature of the company's investors or its debt level—because without it, eventually a company will die, especially if it's not getting access to a lot of capital by selling stock. They might have just a few investors taking on all the risk and hoping for a reward. Startups and younger companies can have negative profitability—a net loss—for quite a while as they build and grow, running the company off of early invested capital. But mature companies need to earn a profit to grow and thrive.

Given what we shared about Apple's cash position and cash flow in the last chapter, it won't surprise you to learn that it's one of the most profitable companies in the world. But don't let that make you think that profit and cash flow are the same.

Cash flow is simply the difference between actual cash received and actual cash used in the process of doing business during a specific period. Net income or profit, you might remember, is the starting point for determining cash flow from operating activities. But because of accrual-based accounting methods, profit doesn't tell us how much cash has been actually generated. Profit is revenue from the sale of services and products that has been recorded—*regardless of whether payment has been received yet or not*—minus all the expenses that have been recorded—*regardless of whether they've been paid or not.*

When you sell a product or service to a customer, your accounting team records that sale and the dollar amount shows up in your company's accounts as revenue. That revenue feeds into the income or profit that shows up in the accounts and the company's income statement. Your customer might not pay that invoice for 30 or 60 days, or might pay gradually over a year or more, but the profit on the "books" includes the total dollar amount anyway.

While you could say that the profit isn't "real" because the cash hasn't moved in and out of the company, it's still important to know whether a company is earning a profit from its core business, making more than it's spending, over a period of time. If we didn't calculate profit this way, a company could appear to not earn any income one month, be hugely profitable the next, and so on, depending on when its own bills are due and when its customers pay their invoices. But that wouldn't be a very good indicator of how consistently it's earning income from its core operations, would it?

All things being equal, a profitable company is healthier than an unprofitable company. An even better sign of health is key revenue and profit measures trending up while expenses *as a percent of sales* trend down over time. This is what company leaders and investors look for. It shows that a company has staying power, that it can continue to take advantage of opportunities to grow, to improve its products and services, to weather tough economic conditions in the future because it's continuing to operate its core business better and more efficiently over time.

Consequently, profit is almost always a primary factor in company strategy and can become the main focus, especially if profits have been somewhat flat or declining. That's why it's so important as a salesperson to understand how profitable your clients are, what decisions they make to *grow* their profitability, and how your products and services can support their profit-growth strategies.

How Companies Become More Profitable

There are two fundamental levers companies pull on to increase profits.

Grow Revenue   Companies grow sales revenue by increasing the *price* of goods or services they sell or increasing the *volume* of goods and services they sell—or even both! Understanding how you can help your customers do either one is key to your success. But keep in mind that while you're trying to sell more to your customers, maintaining or even increasing the price point of your offerings is important to your *own* company's profitability.

People might be willing to pay a higher price for a product if the perceived value has been boosted through enhanced features or better support or if market demand is driving the price up. For a higher value example, consider the price of smartphones versus the most basic cell phones. For market demand, just look at the astronomical price of Taylor Swift's Eras Tour tickets or the cost of an Uber ride when you walk out of the stadium after a playoff game.

However, increasing the price might turn customers off—a situation you may be all too familiar with. The result could be *more* profit earned on each product sold, but *less* total revenue and profit. Imagine the restaurant you go to the most increased its prices by 30%. Would you go as often? If you've got a strict "dining out" budget, probably not. You might even reduce your visits so much that overall, they're getting less of your money, not more. If enough customers are turned off, they might suddenly find that their dining room is empty. But some companies use premium pricing as a strategy, and it works for them. Louis Vuitton, Apple, and lululemon all have strong pricing power because of high demand, and their high prices haven't hurt their total revenue.

Companies use all kinds of strategies to increase the *volume* of their sales, especially marketing, improving the skills of their sales team (there's a reason you're reading this book!), changing their goods and services, and even *lowering* their prices to increase demand. We often see price wars across different industries. Ikea is known for dropping the price on its older products. In March 2024, a time when so many retailers had increased their prices due to inflation, Ikea cut prices on hundreds of products—which earned it lots of positive news coverage and probably higher sales volumes. They may have reduced their profitability on each product sold, but by pulling people into their stores, they might have boosted revenue and profit overall.

Reduce Expenses   As a salesperson, you might have a visceral negative reaction to the phrase "reducing expenses." Your job is to help your company grow revenue, and that might put you in a "grow, grow, grow" mindset. But what you probably hear from your clients a lot is how focused they are on controlling costs. They might try to squeeze every dollar out of your negotiations.

We like to explain why with the phrase **100 up, 100 down**: If a company sells a lot more of its products and generates $100,000 more in revenue, it still has to make and distribute the products, pay salaries and commissions to the employees involved, and pay taxes. In the end, it's left with just a bit of profit from that revenue, maybe $10,000. But if it *reduces expenses or costs* by $100,000, almost all of that money flows down into profit: $100,000 reduction up, $100,000 increase down. It's not quite that perfect, because as profit increases so do taxes, but you get the point.

So when you can connect your offerings to expense reductions elsewhere, you can boost your value proposition.

One of our favorite examples of reducing expenses also comes from UPS. The biggest costs for the company are labor—their delivery drivers—and maintaining their fleet of 100,000-plus trucks. They want to make sure that the cost of delivering each package is as low as possible and that they're using their assets as efficiently as possible (more on this in the next chapter), so they invested in a GPS system called Orion. They used it to analyze different truck routing patterns and discovered that left-hand turns increased drive time and accounted for 70% of the accidents across their fleet. The best solution was to avoid left-hand turns if at all possible in their truck route planning. That one strategy reduced the number of trucks they needed in their fleet and saved time, fuel costs, repair costs, workers' compensation, and more—to the tune of about *$400 million a year.*

There are lots of expenses in any company, so there are lots of opportunities to make cuts or have an impact on costs without putting the burden on one particular area. However, there's an old adage in business: *You can't cut your way to growth.* First, some costs can't be controlled in the short term, like rent. But more important, if a company isn't careful, it can cut costs so much that it reduces the quality of the products and services it offers. Then, customers stop buying, revenue drops, the company can't invest in growth, and eventually it can fail.

Let's look at the three basic categories of expenses or costs to see where and how a company might make smart reductions. Start thinking about how you can align your sales approach with them.

Cost of goods sold (COGS), cost of sales, or cost of services: These are the costs *directly* associated with the production or sale of products or services and are usually variable based on how much of a product or service a company sells. Cost of goods sold for a company that manufactures delivery trucks, for instance, would include things like raw materials such as steel and computer chips and the factory labor to manufacture the trucks. Cost of goods sold for the computer chip manufacturer would include silicon. Walmart's cost of sales would include the wholesale price it pays the original manufacturer of each item it sells. Cost of services at a law firm would be the cost of the lawyers working a particular case. Apple tracks costs of goods sold but also costs of services for all the repairs they perform.

Companies might try to reduce COGS by negotiating lower prices with suppliers, improving their manufacturing process to reduce waste or scrap, and improving efficiency to reduce time and labor. Lowering COGS too much can result in lower-quality products or services that lead to lost sales revenue or even recall expenses, so companies have to be careful.

Operating expenses: Operating costs—also known as overhead, fixed costs, or indirect costs—are costs associated with running the business that may not feed directly into the creation of goods or services.

Common operating expenses include research and development (R&D) and a blanket category called selling, general, and administrative (SG&A). SG&A includes salaries, rent, advertising costs, utilities, and so on. Service-based businesses, like UPS, might focus on operating costs rather than cost of sales or COGS.

The big challenge is that these costs tend to be more fixed and harder to reduce when a company goes through a period of lower sales and revenue. One way to dramatically reduce operating costs that gets a lot of press is through layoffs. It's not ideal if the downturn is temporary, and leaders have to factor in the impact on the company's culture and its product and service quality. A better option is reducing waste of all types—in materials or productivity. That's what UPS did with their left-turn strategy, right? That said, in 2023, when its sales took a downward turn and expenses rose, they did resort to layoffs.

Walmart is also known for its strict cost controls: It's relentless in its negotiation with buyers, it combines shipments so trucks only drive with full loads, and executives are expected to fly coach when they travel.

Interest and taxes: Companies face financing costs—especially interest on loans—that are difficult to control, except when they can renegotiate the terms. They have a bit more opportunity when it comes to taxes. As they increase profit, they also increase their taxable income, which means higher federal, state, and local taxes. But if a company reinvests its profits into the development of the business and takes advantage of tax breaks wherever it can, it lowers its tax liability and the money saved increases its profit dollar for dollar.

Companies are always looking for opportunities to drive efficiency and innovate in order to control costs and stay competitive. But if a company wants to continue to grow its profits, it has to both increase revenues and control costs.

THE IMPORTANT PROFIT MEASURES

Now, we're going to walk you through some common profit measures. You'll see them on financial statements and in the news, and understand-

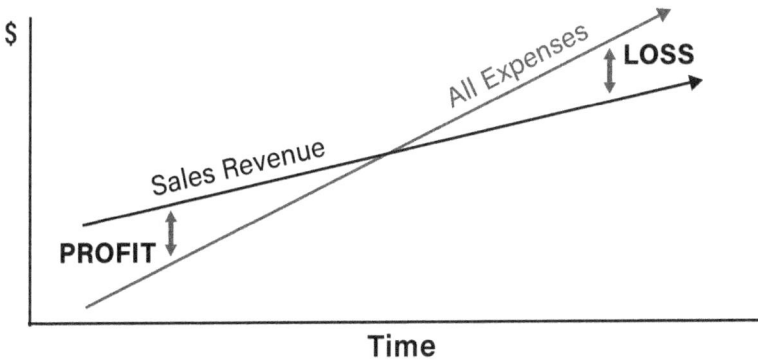

ing them will help you hone your business acumen, better understand your customer, talk in terms that executives appreciate, and improve the power of your value proposition.

Revenue or Sales

Remember that profit is revenue minus expenses, so revenue alone isn't a profit measure, but you can't calculate other profit measures without it! And knowing the total revenue of a company and how it's changing over time, especially compared to profit, tells you a lot about the company's future.

Total revenue, the top line, or simply *revenue* is pretty straightforward: the dollar value of goods and services sold as a result of a company's normal business activities. Usually when people talk about how a company is growing, especially if they're saying it grew by x or y percent, they're talking about growth in total revenue. As a salesperson, you directly contribute to revenue and its growth for your company! The question is, can you find a way to impact your client's revenue.

Gross Profit or Income

Gross profit is calculated by subtracting the direct cost of goods sold or the cost of sales from total revenue. Gross profit is important because it tells you how efficiently a company is producing and selling its products.

Leaders will look at gross profit as they set prices, decide whether to sell a product or service, determine the product and service mix they'll offer, and decide how much money they should budget for buying or making a product. Often, they'll go granular with this number and determine the gross profit from each good sold—each chip manufactured, each truck built—because they want to earn as much as possible from *each* sale. Remember, profit from core business operations is the best kind of profit, because the company earned it!

Operating Profit or Income

Operating profit is calculated by subtracting all operating expenses—indirect costs—from gross profit. For companies that don't track cost of goods sold or gross profit separately, operating costs are subtracted from total revenue. As we wrote above, service companies, like UPS, may not record cost of goods sold and may only show operating profit. But for some companies, you'll see a mix of gross profit and operating profit in their financial reports. What's important to know is every company ultimately wants to earn as much as possible from its core business operations, a key opportunity for you. At the very least, a company's operating profit should be positive. It should be covering the cost of operating its core business from what it sells.

Net Profit or Income

Most companies have expenses—and income—beyond their core operations. Remember the other activities that businesses engage in that we described in the last chapter: financing activities and investing activities. Most large companies have debts that they're paying interest on, and they may be earning income from investments. Finally, they also have taxes that need to be paid. When you add these other sources of income and subtract these other types of expenses you get net profit, which can also be called net income, net earnings, profit for the year, or a company's bottom line.

THREE KINDS OF PROFIT

» Gross profit tells how profitable a company's products or services are.

» Operating profit tells you how profitable the company's day-to-day operations are.

» Net profit tells you how profitable the whole enterprise is.

Profit Margin

A company's profit margin isn't usually handed to you in a financial report. It requires a bit of math, because it's a percentage—income or profit as a percent of total revenue:

$$\frac{\text{Profit (or Income)}}{\text{Revenue}} \times 100 = \text{Profit Margin (\%)}$$

You can use this same basic equation to calculate gross profit margin, operating profit margin, or net profit margin. What does the number mean? If net profit margin is 10%, which is actually average for most large companies, then 10 cents out of every dollar received is profit. Remember, context for these numbers is important. In the retail industry, profit margins tend to be fairly low, while they tend to be much higher in the tech industry.

Why do leaders or analysts care about margins? Because they tell us how *efficiently* a company is turning revenue into profit. Even though one company has lower profit in dollars than another, its profit margin might be significantly higher, indicating a well-managed business that generates more profit from every dollar of revenue. But a margin that's much lower than the industry average or the average for the size of the company means the company might be facing tough times. The exception is when they are reinvesting potential profits into the company as part of a growth strategy.

Earnings per Share

Publicly traded companies track earnings per share, which tells you how much profit (earnings) was generated for each share of stock. It's calculated by dividing net income by the number of shares of common stock outstanding. It's one of the most important drivers of stock price. You can bet the leaders of any publicly traded company have a close eye on it. Anything you can do to impact your company's or your clients' profitability will positively impact EPS.

LEVERAGING PROFIT IN THE SALES PROCESS

Savvy salesperson Lucas, from the start of the chapter, understood how to talk about profitability with his client. Specifically, he talked about how his product could help them reduce expenses overall and improve profitability. As a salesperson, you can do the same. Let's come back to UPS to understand how.

We've explained why 2022 was a year worth celebrating for UPS. But one year later, things were much less rosy. Leaders saw the writing on the wall when their net income for the very first quarter of 2023 was lower than they had predicted. Let's take a look at what Carol Tomé, the CEO, had to say when they shared their quarterly reports with the world.

"Deceleration in U.S. retail sales resulted in lower volume than we anticipated, and we faced ongoing demand weakness in Asia."[8] *Translation:* Our revenue was lower this quarter, compared to previous quarters, because we didn't sell as much of our service—the volume of packages we handled was lower. If you were selling to UPS, this might be a red flag—unless you could help the company boost sales, for instance by breaking into another market or improving its competitiveness against FedEx.

"In response, we focused on controlling what we could control and delivered first-quarter consolidated operating profit and operating [profit] margin in line with our base case targets." *Translation:* We reduced costs where we could to balance out the loss of revenue, so our profit numbers didn't drop as much as they could have. They're obviously cost-conscious, so any value proposition you come to them with should have a clear cost-savings component.

"Given current macro conditions, we expect volume to remain under pressure. We will remain focused on driving productivity while investing in efficiency and growth initiatives, enabling us to come out of this demand cycle even stronger." *Translation:* We think our revenue is going to continue to be lower than we'd like [and they were right] so we're going to stay focused on controlling expenses and generating as much profit as possible based on those expenses: efficiency and productivity. More right turns! We'll explore assets and making the best use of them in the next chapter, but anything you can do to connect to their desire to operate as efficiently as possible now and strengthen their operations in the long term would get their attention.

UPS is a helpful example, but what are we really saying about leveraging profit in the sales process?

First, consider how you could help your client improve their top line or revenue. This is especially important if you've learned that it has been flat or even declining. How could you help them add value to their products and services that could increase demand and the volume they sell or allow them to reasonably increase the price? If you sell customer communication software, you can help your client provide better service. If you sell microchips, you can help them improve the processing speed of their products. Is there something you offer that could help them reach a new kind of customer or move into a different market by making slight changes to their goods or services?

If your client thinks they can't increase prices without hurting demand, you might look at helping them improve sales volume through strategies like the following:

- Helping them innovate their products and services to create new offerings that are more profitable or in higher demand.

- Helping them improve their marketing and customer management to drive demand for products.

- Helping them improve how they sell online or go after new distribution channels.

- Helping them move into new markets, geographically or demographically.

Next, pay close attention to their profit and profit margins, especially if any profit margin is running below the industry norm (see Resource 3) or has been declining. Remember, you represent an expense for them, so you may want to focus on how investing in your product or service can save them money elsewhere. As we explained, even if you can help grow their revenue, they'll care more about controlling costs and improving their margin. Consider these two questions:

- Does your product or service help customers reduce specific costs? Exactly how does it do that, and what are the typical results?

- Does your product or service help consolidate certain operations to eliminate wasted time or effort or materials?

Regardless of how you can help your clients be more profitable, be prepared to talk about it in real terms. Show your knowledge of what their current results mean for the company, how they might be influencing the company's decisions and strategies, and show that you're thinking about how you can contribute.

To help you gather the information you need to make these value propositions land, we'll look at the income statement next. If you primarily sell to privately held companies, you may not have access to their income statement, but you may be able to gather information about their profitability in other ways. For instance, you can find some information in business news sources. HEB, a grocery company based in Texas, is on the Forbes list of largest privately held companies, where they publish their revenue. Regardless of where you find it, what matters more is what you do with whatever information you can gather to grow your partnership with customers.

THE INCOME STATEMENT

The purpose of an income statement—also called a profit and loss statement, a statement of earnings, a P&L, or a statement of operations—is to show whether a company made or lost money during the reporting period, whether it generated a profit or a loss. It's based on the profit equation we described above:

Revenue - Expenses = Profit

Think about an income statement like climbing down a ladder. The top rung, or the top line, is your revenue or sales. Then you have a bunch of rungs that represent different costs or expenses and a few special sources of income. Finally, the bottom rung, or the bottom line, reveals your net income or profit—how much you made after you subtracted all your expenses and added any other income. Even though all income statements follow this flow, they can look quite different, especially for companies in different industries or with different business models. So we're going to show you two examples. We're going to start with NVIDIA, a chip manufacturing company and computing innovator that has generated amazing profit margins, and then we're going to return to UPS and their story.

INCOME STATEMENT DECODER RING

- » Revenue *AKA* sales, net sales or net revenues, top line
- » Cost of goods sold (COGS) *AKA* cost of revenue, cost of sales
- » Operating income *AKA* operating profit, earnings before income and taxes (EBIT) (not technically the same as operating income, but often close in value)
- » Net income *AKA* profit or net profit, net earnings, bottom line

NVIDIA's Consolidated Income Statement

(in millions, except per share data)

	Years Ended		
	Jan 26, 2025	Jan 28, 2024	Jan 29, 2023
Revenue	$ 130,497	$ 60,922	$ 26,974
Cost of revenue	32,639	16,621	11,618
Gross profit	97,858	44,301	15,356
Operating expenses			
Research and development	12,914	8,675	7,339
Sales, general and administrative	3,491	2,654	2,440
Acquisition termination cost	—	—	1,353
Total operating expenses	16,405	11,329	11,132
Operating income	81,453	32,972	4,224
Interest income	1,786	866	267
Interest expense	(247)	(257)	(262)
Other, net	1,034	237	(48)
Other income (expense), net	2,573	846	(43)
Income before income tax	84,026	33,818	4,181
Income tax expense (benefit)	11,146	4,058	(187)
Net income	$ 72,880	$ 29,760	$ 4,368
Net income per share:			
Basic	$ 2.97	$ 1.21	$ .18
Diluted	$ 2.94	$ 1.19	$ .17
Weighted average shares used in per-share computation:			
Basic	24,555	24,690	24,870
Diluted	24,804	24,940	25,070

We've highlighted the important numbers for you to make it easier to navigate through the profit measures. For their 2025 fiscal year, NVIDIA recorded:

- revenue of over $130 billion
- gross profit of almost $98 billion
- operating income or profit of over $81 billion
- net income or profit of $72.9 billion
- earnings per share (EPS) of $2.94—leaders typically refer to diluted EPS rather than basic EPS, and while the difference doesn't matter much, you can learn more about the two at SellingtheBigPicture.com.

When you compare these numbers to the previous year and calculate NVIDIA's margins—profit divided by revenue—the numbers are impressive. Remember, context and trends matter. NVIDIA's revenue more than doubled in one year. That's a big feat for a large company. But much, much more impressive is that their net income increased 145%! And their net profit margin is almost 56%! Remember, the average for most large, public companies is 10%. That's astounding. It's not surprising that one of their greatest operating expenses is R&D. Being innovative is how they've cornered the market and grown so fast.

Now let's look at UPS. Doing a quick assessment of its income statement for 2023, we see:

- revenue of over $91 billion
- operating profit of more than $8 billion
- net income or profit of over $5.7 billion
- earnings per share (EPS) of $6.75

UPS's Consolidated Income Statement

(in millions)

	Years Ended December 31,		
	2024	2023	2022
Revenue	$ 91,070	$ 90,958	$ 100,338
Operating expenses:			
Compensation and benefits	48,093	47,088	47,781
Repairs and maintenance	2,940	2,828	2,515
Depreciation and amortization	3,609	3,366	3,188
Purchased transportation	13,589	13,651	17,653
Fuel	4,366	4,775	6,018
Other occupancy	2,117	2,019	1,818
Other expenses	7,888	8,090	8,271
Total operating expenses	82,602	81,817	87,244
Operating profit	8,468	9,141	13,094
Other income and expenses:			
Investment income (expense) and other	(160)	217	2,435
Interest expense	(866)	(785)	(704)
Total other income and expenses	(1,026)	(568)	1,731
Income before income taxes	7,442	8,573	14,825
Income tax expense	1,660	1,865	3,277
Net income	$ 5,782	$ 6,708	$ 11,548
Basic earnings per share	$ 6.76	$ 7.81	$ 13.26
Diluted earnings per share	$ 6.75	$ 7.80	$ 13.20

If you climb down the ladder of UPS's income statement, you'll see their major expenses. For instance, repairs and maintenance and fuel, which they reduced with their no left turns strategy. Many of the rungs on the ladder might be self-explanatory, but depreciation and amortization is a bit more complex. Let's spend a minute demystifying them. They're simply a way of accounting for two basic costs: 1. Depreciation spreads the cost of the asset over its useful life. Given UPS's huge fleet of trucks and planes, it has big depreciation costs. And it has to continually invest in new trucks to replace the old ones. That cost increased in January 2024, when UPS began investing in air conditioning in its new trucks. 2. Amortization helps spread the cost of purchasing an intangible asset, like a software license, over time.

If you're selling expensive equipment or software, it's important to know that no matter when your client pays for your solution, the cost will show up in their accounts in increments over years, following specific IRS rules. That can be in your favor, especially for public companies that have to report profit every quarter and don't want a massive expense tanking that number.

Remember, it's important to look at the trends and relationships between numbers. For instance,

- UPS had been on a positive trend in revenue and *operating* profit before both fell dramatically in 2023, as we've already described. Operating profit fell again in 2024, while revenue increased slightly.

- Net income or total profit fell each year shown in the statement, from $11.5 billion in 2022 all the way down to $5.8 billion in 2024. Revenue fell by about $9.5 billion in 2023, a drop of about 9%. *But net income fell by almost 42%.* That resulted in a big drop in EPS, and you can be sure leaders were very concerned. Which is why they took the immediate actions we described in the last section.

- Even though net income fell substantially, it still fell less in *dollar amounts* than revenue, and that has a lot to do with UPS's efforts to control operating costs. If they hadn't taken such a big hit in their investment income, their net income and net profit margin, which was 7.4% for 2023, would have looked even better.

- In 2024, revenue picked up again, but net income still fell. Why? One big factor was higher compensation and benefit costs as a result of the agreement UPS reached with workers at the end of 2023 to avoid a strike.

Changes like these in total revenue, net income, and profit margins are what you want to hunt for when you're looking at your clients' income statements. They represent opportunities to better understand their goals, their challenges, upcoming initiatives, shifts in their core business, and more. It doesn't take much reading between the lines to find opportunities to align your sales approach with their needs and targets.

› › › › › *PROFIT IN REVIEW*

» Profit, which is also called income or earnings, is the difference between the revenue a company generates (and that you help generate for your company!) by selling goods and services and the expenses it incurs to create and sell them.

» Investors evaluate the worth of companies primarily by their potential to consistently increase profit over time, which means companies are always looking for ways to grow their revenue or reduce their costs.

» Companies can increase revenue by raising prices or selling more products to the same or new customers. They can reduce costs primarily by decreasing the direct costs of producing and selling their products, called cost of goods sold or cost of revenue or sales, or by reducing their operating expenses, which include fixed costs like rent, salaries, and other "overhead." Sometimes they can also reduce their tax burden to help boost their bottom line.

» The important measures are:

  · Total revenue

  · Gross profit—revenue less cost of goods sold or cost of revenue

  · Operating profit—revenue *or* gross profit less all operating expenses

  · Net profit—revenue less *all* costs, including operating costs, financing and investment costs, taxes, and other costs

  · Profit margin (gross, operating, or net)—profit divided by revenue, shown as a percentage

- Earnings per share (EPS)—net income divided by the number of shares of common stock outstanding

» Because profit is so vital, especially in public companies, it represents a big sales opportunity. Anything you can do to connect your products and services to benefits that help your customers grow their sales—by helping them innovate, improve marketing, improve customer satisfaction, improve how they sell online, or break into new markets—is a big plus. And given that you represent an expense for your customers, anything you can do to show how your offerings can reduce other expenses or operate more efficiently will make them happy.

» You can find the important profit numbers on the income statement, which is also called the profit and loss statement or the P&L. Even though the general structure is always the same, with revenue at the top and net income or profit at the bottom and a host of expenses in between, income statements can look a bit different between industries and business models.

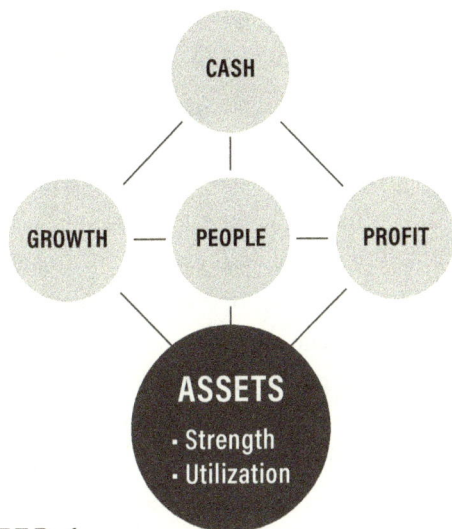

CHAPTER 4

ASSETS

"Apple has some tremendous assets, but I believe without
some attention, the company could, could, could—I'm
searching for the right word—could, could die."[9]
—Steve Jobs, on his return as interim CEO in 1997

IMAGINE IF WALMART HAD WAREHOUSES FULL OF goods that
weren't selling or that it didn't know how much of any product it might
need at a specific store. Even for those of us not in retail, that sounds
disastrous. No retailer, especially one that's usually sitting on more than
$50 *billion* worth of inventory, like Walmart often is, wants their inven-
tory sitting in a warehouse or on store shelves and not selling. It's why
they call it "dead money."

Luckily, Matias understood that. His company developed AI-driven
sales and inventory management solutions ideal for retailers. And he
knew that their core product was stronger than the competitor's in one
important way: predictive analytics. It gave real-time, accurate data
on all current inventory at a granular level, and even better, produced

reports that accurately predicted upcoming inventory needs by month and quarter. With better forecasting, a company could improve its ordering accuracy and not buy stock that wasn't going to sell quickly.

Matias was prepared to talk about all of this as he began a presentation for the operations team of a new potential client. He walked them through the system, focusing on how the software could improve the company's inventory planning and analysis, sharing cases from similar companies, and even calculating the impact of better inventory management on the company's revenue, profit, and cash flow—the *return on investment* the company could earn with his software. And when he described the overall *asset utilization* improvement for the company, the more senior leaders were immediately interested.

Matias had a signed contract in his inbox a month later.

Every company and every one of us owns assets. Your house, your car, your cash savings, your investments are all assets. You might not use your house to produce revenue or profit, but your savings and investments *do* produce income for you. Likewise, companies own assets they either use to generate revenue and profit or that they hold onto or save in case of financial trouble in the future, like the cash Apple has accumulated. The first option is called *asset utilization*. The second option feeds a company's *asset strength*.

Without enough assets or the right combination of assets, a company can't remain in business; it can't be profitable. It sells its inventory of products to generate revenue. It leases or buys office space to create space for employees, warehouses to store products, and plants to manufacture goods. It uses transportation assets, like shipping containers and trucks, to get its products to customers. It uses cash assets to pay bills, to make investments, and to buy supplies, materials, and equipment. Now, some items that we might think of as assets don't show up on any financial statements, even though they're an important part of how a company produces revenue and profit. For example, customer relationships and a company's employees. People are so important, though, that we consider them to be an entirely separate driver.

The big challenge for all leaders is balancing their asset strength with asset utilization. On the one hand, they need to hold onto assets like cash that don't yield much income to have resources in case of trouble *or* to take advantage of opportunities that crop up. On the other hand, they need to use their assets today to invest in production plants, purchase equipment, or even acquire other businesses in order to produce even greater revenue and profit in the short and long term. They're constantly asking: Do we have enough assets, of the right kind, and are we using them as well as we could to grow the company?

Like Matias, you might be influencing the answers. Every time a company buys from you, it's potentially reducing its asset strength so that it can invest in assets it hopes will help it earn more revenue, improve cash flow, and increase profit. It's your job to show your clients how this could happen. This chapter will help put you in the mindset of your clients, help you understand how they perceive products and services as assets, and help you describe the benefit of your offerings long past the end of the sales cycle.

So let's look at asset strength and utilization more closely.

ASSET STRENGTH: WEATHERING STORMS

Suppose you, as an individual, have plenty of cash in savings, investments of different types, good equity in your home (all assets), and very little debt. You're more likely to survive financially during a downturn or if you lost your job, aren't you? The same principle is true of companies.

If somebody asked you, "How strong is this company?" you might think about cash flow or profit, but if you're speaking to a potential investor or analyst, they would also be interested in asset strength. **Asset strength is a strong indicator of overall financial health. Why? Because a company can rely on its assets in times of trouble.**

Imagine a major downturn in the economy that cuts a company's cash flow and profits by 30% to 50%. For instance, a pandemic. Can the company survive in the short term, when it may have enough cash on hand to help, and also in the longer term? Can it cover its operating expenses, like rent or salaries? Can it cover its loan payments? A company's asset strength reflects its ability to meet its financial obligations, now and in the future, to survive the storms and fluctuations of business, *and* to take advantage of profitable opportunities when they arise. It manages these feats of strength by possessing cash and other assets of greater value than its liabilities—its debts and future financial obligations.

Because asset strength is so important, leaders, investors, and analysts examine it from multiple angles.

- **Liquidity:** Liquidity is the ability to get quick access to cash. By definition, cash is the most liquid asset. The more liquid a business is, the more cash it has readily available or can generate, quickly and without much cost. With more cash on hand and cash equivalents, a company can buy or invest in other types of assets—like investing in its manufacturing capacity, upgrading IT, or buying other businesses—to make money. This is especially important during times of economic uncertainty.

- **Equity:** Equity is simply the total value of a company's assets minus the total amount of its debts and other financial obligations, like contracts it signed that require it to make future payments. Those obligations are its liabilities. Just like the equity in your home—its market value minus what you owe on your mortgage—the equity of a business represents a reserve it can tap into if it needs cash. For instance, just as you could take out a home equity loan, a company can borrow against the equity in its assets.

- **Ability to cover debts:** Leaders, accountants, and analysts are also concerned with a company's ability to cover its financial obligations in the short term. Stronger companies can pay their bills for a year and still have liquid assets left over. If a company has just enough liquid assets on hand to cover itself for 12 months, its asset strength may be shaky. If revenue suddenly drops, or a big customer delays paying, a company may have trouble making payments. And if a compelling opportunity to invest in growth suddenly crops up, it may not be able to take advantage of it.

Credit rating agencies such as Standard & Poor's (S&P) and Moody's use all this information, plus profit, cash flow, and in-depth analysis of other financial information, to assess the risk to investors of lending money to or purchasing stock in companies. The greater the asset strength of a company, the less risky it is because it has resources to fall back on in times of trouble. A strong credit rating and the ability to readily borrow money might tell you a lot about a potential customer's decision-making process or your likelihood of closing a big contract.

ASSET UTILIZATION: GENERATING RETURNS

Again, asset utilization tells us how effectively and efficiently a company is using its assets to generate more revenue and reduce costs to increase profit. The biggest factor in determining asset utilization is productivity: the amount of work accomplished or goods produced per unit of assets used.

Measuring asset productivity is a science. There are so many different types of assets, and you need different types of measures to determine how productive each asset is. For instance, how you measure the productivity of a marketing employee is substantially different from how you measure the productivity of a widget machine. And many companies, especially manufacturing companies, need to understand in fine detail how productive each asset is to make sure they are investing wisely and using each asset to maximize the return on those investments.

As a salesperson, you should understand how your clients assess the productivity of any asset you're selling, so let's take a look at a few examples.

We shared the UPS "no left turn" story in the last chapter, but it's also a great example of improving the productivity of two assets—its fleet of trucks and its drivers. Another great example comes from Delta. For many years, planes were positioned perpendicular to the terminal, pushed straight back away from the gate by a tug, and then turned 90 degrees to get aligned with the taxiway. Planes couldn't start their engines until that point.

But then, some savvy employees, customer service agents, proposed a different process. Why not push the planes back at a 45-degree angle? This one simple change cut seconds off every gate departure and allowed planes to start their engines almost a minute sooner. This meant fewer delays across the fleet through saved time, better position in the take-off queue, and generally faster takeoffs. Airlines measure the utilization of airplanes in block hours. Block hours for a given flight is the time from the moment the aircraft pushes back from the departure gate until the moment the aircraft arrives at the arrival gate. This simple change helped reduce that number.

Compare that boost to what happened in July 2024, when the cyber-security company CrowdStrike put out a faulty update for its Falcon Sensor software. The update caused more than eight million Microsoft-based systems to crash, creating huge problems across multiple industries. Delta was especially hard hit. The company had to cancel more than 5,000 flights over a five-day period, and according to CEO Ed Bastian, it cost Delta more than $500 million. Imagine all of those airplanes sitting on the tarmac, not being put to use to earn revenue or profit.

Airlines think about asset utilization one way, and other industries think about it in very different terms. For instance, later in this chapter, we'll share information about inventory turnover, which is a vital utilization measure for retailers. The big takeaway, though, is to make sure you understand how the specific industries and companies you sell to assess asset utilization so that you can speak to their goals and understand their strategies.

Balancing Strength and Utilization

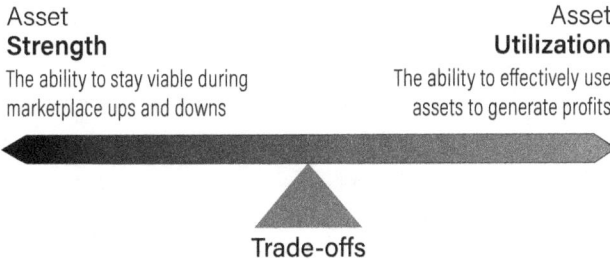

Asset	Asset
Strength	**Utilization**
The ability to stay viable during	The ability to effectively use
marketplace ups and downs	assets to generate profits

Trade-offs

LEVERAGING ASSETS IN THE SALES PROCESS

Some of the greatest companies in the world are great because they chose to reach beyond their competitors and invest in assets that would help them grow in the future—help them access new markets, help them create unimagined products, help them solve a problem never solved before. And every company is interested in making better and better use of the assets it already has. If you can help your customers make these decisions, you'll be in great shape to close more sales.

Understanding Return on Investment

How do businesspeople determine whether to spend money to acquire a particular asset, especially given that they have a lot of opportunities to do so? And each opportunity might mean giving up some of their asset strength or liquidity. The best decisions are those that provide more income and profit in the future, even more than the amount of assets invested—they produce a return on investment (ROI). The better the ROI, the better the investment. Determining ROI for individual projects can help businesspeople successfully balance asset strength and utilization, and actually drive both.

As a salesperson, your primary role will be to show a likely return on investment for any investment in assets you're asking your

customer to make. It should help the company generate more revenue or income or help it reduce costs so that it achieves higher profit. At a minimum it should generate a return greater than the interest paid on the loan to buy the assets, or a greater return than the interest that could have been earned on the cash if they kept it in a savings account.

How do you measure ROI? Typically, the income or profit produced by any asset divided by its cost is the ROI for that asset. However, ROI can be measured in many ways: Retailers, for example, might measure annual sales per square foot of their stores. **Ultimately, calculating ROI comes down to *cost-benefit analysis*.** To do this type of analysis, first determine the costs of the opportunity or investment to be made (cash, labor costs, the cost of running a machine, etc.), and then assess the *benefits* to be gained (revenue, cost reduction, or product value that could be created). Then, divide the benefit by the cost to calculate the percentage return on the investment.

$$\frac{\text{Return, or Benefit}}{\text{Investment, or Cost}} \times 100 = \text{ROI (\%)}$$

Identifying the benefits of alternative options through ROI analysis is an extremely important application of business acumen. When you do this analysis for your customers, it can help them understand how your product is a better investment than, say, a competitor's product, or even an older version of your own product. Recall the story of Lucas from the previous chapter, who showed his pharmaceutical client that the extra cost of the new shipping containers could produce a better return on investment because of the reduced shipping costs.

How Can You Contribute to Better Asset Utilization?

A machine making 100 widgets per day is more productive, and is being better utilized, than a similar widget machine making only 50 per day. And if your product or service can help make those machines more productive, you're in a strong sales position. Consider how you—and the products or services you're selling—can play a role in identifying, reducing, or eliminating prospective clients' underperforming assets and replacing them with more efficient ones.

Stretch your mind a little as you look for creative ways your offerings can help clients maximize asset productivity and the returns the assets generate. Kingsford, the leading manufacturer of charcoal in the United States, was founded when Henry Ford learned of a way to turn the wood scraps from automobile floorboards into charcoal briquettes. Ford in effect converted the waste from one asset into an asset in its own right!

One great way is to look at how your product or service contributes to reduction in the cycle time of a business process, which increases productivity, saves people time, reduces costs, and generally makes better use of assets. This is often called business process improvement. McDonald's is known as *the* innovator in standardized, efficient processes that have become fast-food industry norms. Anywhere you go in the world, you will find that a Big Mac and the process for making and serving it are virtually the same. That work has helped them reduce costs, increase profit, and improve their asset utilization.

No matter what you are selling, if you can talk to your customers about how it can help them improve the productivity of their assets and their overall return on assets (especially when talking to anybody in the C-suite), you'll be closer to a signed deal.

THE IMPORTANT ASSET MEASURES

When you're talking to senior leaders, using their language to address asset strength and utilization will help you connect and prove your credibility. So let's look at the measures most commonly used when assessing or making decisions about assets.

Equity Ratio

When it comes to asset strength, an important place to start is with shareholders' equity, also called *stockholders' equity* or *net assets*. It's the difference between total assets and total liabilities. Again, a company's assets include everything they *own or control* that has economic value. Liabilities are debts a company *owes*. Shareholders' equity is what the owners or shareholders would have left after selling all of the assets and paying off all the liabilities.

The *equity ratio* is the total shareholders' equity divided by total assets, expressed as a percentage:

$$\frac{\text{Total shareholders' equity}}{\text{Total assets}} \times 100 = \text{equity ratio}$$

What it reflects is how well a company is managing its debt. The average equity ratio for the S&P 500 is about 33%. A higher ratio means that a company has more equity to borrow against if needed, making it a better credit risk and probably more capable of borrowing more money if it needed to. The ability to borrow money is an important factor in the potential growth of a company.

Current Ratio

Remember how important it is to understand a company's ability to cover its debts and other financial obligations? The current ratio is an important measure for assessing that piece of the asset strength puzzle. It is simply the current assets divided by the current liabilities. Current assets are those the company expects to convert to cash within 12 months, and current liabilities are those due to be paid within the next 12 months.

From your perspective as a salesperson, one reason to pay attention to the current ratio is if your company offers financing. Is a client a good financing candidate? Or are they carrying too much current debt right now—debt they might have a hard time covering if there was a sudden negative change in their business?

If the current ratio is greater than 1, which is typically what you want to see in larger public companies, it means that the company is more likely to meet their financial obligations—including payments for anything you sell to them! If the ratio is less than 1, the company might have a hard time paying its debts if it hits a rough patch. However, it can vary by industry. The average current ratio for the companies in the S&P 500 is about 1.5, while Walmart's is often below 1. It has such great cash flow, though, that no analyst would consider it a credit risk.

Delta recently made a change that would improve its current ratio—and the backlash from customers was immediate. Loyalty programs like Delta SkyMiles show up as liabilities in a company's financial reports because these programs represent something of financial value that the company owes to its customers. When companies change the value of the points outstanding, by increasing or decreasing what you can get with them, they change their liability level. If it suddenly takes 75,000 miles to buy a ticket rather than 50,000, each point is technically worth less.

In 2023, Delta had a current liability from its loyalty program of $3.9 billion, an increase of $1.2 billion from just two years before, partially due to its partnership with American Express and how easy Delta had made it to earn loyalty points and premium status during the fall-off in travel during the pandemic. Delta decided to change the benefits you can earn through the AmEx partnership, essentially reducing the value of the points outstanding, reducing how fast people could accrue benefits going forward, and thus reducing Delta's liability.

The growing mass of customers at the highest levels revolted, and CEO Ed Bastian had to explain that the current load of high-tier customers and commitments were "just way in excess of our current asset base and it's unsustainable where we're at now."[10] Delta changed course after customer backlash but made it clear that more changes would be coming.

Return on Assets

Determining the productivity of individual assets is important in making day-to-day management decisions. But broader strategic decisions—whether to take on more debt, whether to improve a company's cash position, etc.—may be affected by a company's overall asset utilization. At a high level, asset utilization is measured by *return on assets* (ROA), or the profit generated by the company's assets, as a percentage.

$$\frac{\text{Net income}}{\text{Total assets}} \times 100 = \text{Return on Assets}$$

Remember, the purpose of assets is to increase revenue and profit, which is how a company generates a return for shareholders. The average ROA is quite different by industry and is affected by economic conditions, obviously. That said, the average for the S&P 500 companies is about 8 percent. Generally, and somewhat obviously, the higher the percentage, the better, and anything you can do to improve that number is a good thing—especially by showing how your products or services can help boost profit or net income. This becomes even more important if you're selling high-dollar, enterprise-level solutions that could result in a hit to asset strength. Showing an improvement in asset utilization helps leaders feel that they're making a balanced decision.

Inventory Turnover

Remember the story at the beginning of the chapter about Matias and how he leveraged in? Inventory is a vital asset in many industries, but especially retail. The productivity or utilization of inventory is measured by inventory turnover, or the number of times a company sells through its average inventory in a year. It's cost of goods sold divided by the average cost of inventory on hand.

If a Foot Locker store carries, on average, inventory worth $100,000 in retail sales value, and if its cost of goods sold are $1 million for the year, then it's inventory turnover for the year was 10, meaning it sold through its inventory 10 times over the year. If a competitor has a similar average shoe inventory worth $100,000, but has an inventory turnover of 20, then the competitor sells twice the volume, generates twice the revenue, and generates more profit and cash flow.

Obviously, the higher the inventory turnover the better, because you're earning more money from your assets. Foot Locker's average inventory turnover was 3.91 for 2023, when the average for the retail industry is typically between 5 and 10, one sign of what has caused their fall-off in revenue in recent years. If you sell warehouse or inventory management, customer management, or marketing products and services, this is a good number to know, especially if you can share details about how your offerings can help.

Next, let's turn to the primary source of information about assets—the balance sheet—where you can find what you need to calculate most of these measures.

THE BALANCE SHEET

The balance sheet provides information on assets, liabilities, and equity—factors of a company's asset strength and, along with the income statement and statement of cash flows, indicators of how effectively assets are being utilized to produce a return.

Just like other statements, the balance sheet follows a basic equation:

$$\text{Assets} - \text{Liabilities} = \text{Equity}$$

Keep in mind that only assets a company owns appear on the balance sheet, but it might use many others, such as leased buildings or equipment, to operate its core business.

In the example shown here, for Delta, we've highlighted the key numbers to look at when you're quickly assessing a company based on its balance sheet.

Delta's Consolidated Balance Sheets

(in millions, except share data)

	December 31,		
	2024	2023	2022
ASSETS			
Current Assets:			
Cash and cash equivalents	$ 3,069	$ 2,741	$ 3,266
Short-term investments	—	1,127	3,268
Accounts receivable	3,224	3,130	3,176
Fuel, expendable parts, and supplies inventories	1,428	1,314	1,424
Prepaid expenses and other	2,123	1,957	1,877
Total current assets	**9,844**	**10,269**	**13,011**
Noncurrent Assets:			
Property and equipment, net of accumulated depreciation and amortization	37,595	35,486	33,109
Operating lease right-of-use assets	6,644	7,004	7,036
Goodwill	9,753	9,753	9,753
Identifiable intangibles, net of accumulated amortization	5,975	5,983	5,992
Equity investments	2,846	3,457	2,128
Other noncurrent assets	2,715	1,692	1,259
Total noncurrent assets	65,528	63,375	59,277
Total Assets	**$ 75,372**	**$ 73,644**	**$ 72,288**

	December 31,		
	2024	**2023**	**2022**

LIABILITIES AND STOCKHOLDERS' EQUITY

Current Liabilities:

Current maturities of debt and finance leases	$ 2,175	$ 2,983	$ 2,359
Current maturities of operating leases	763	759	714
Air traffic liability	7,094	7,044	8,160
Accounts payable	4,650	4,446	5,106
Accrued salaries and related benefits	4,762	4,561	3,288
Loyalty program deferred revenue	4,314	3,908	3,434
Fuel card obligation	1,100	1,100	1,100
Other accrued liabilities	1,812	1,617	1,779
Total current liabilities	**26,670**	**26,418**	**25,940**

Noncurrent Liabilities:

Debt and finance leases	14,019	17,071	20,671
Pension, postretirement, and related benefits	3,144	3,601	3,707
Loyalty program deferred revenue	4,512	4,512	4,448
Noncurrent operating leases	5,814	6,468	6,866
Deferred income taxes, net	2,176	908	24
Other noncurrent liabilities	3,744	3,561	4,050
Total noncurrent liabilities	**33,409**	**36,121**	**39,766**

Stockholders' Equity:

Common stock at $0.0001 par value; 1,500,000,000 shares authorized, 654,571,606 and 654,671,194 shares issued	—	—	—
Additional paid-in capital	11,740	11,641	11,526
Retained earnings/(deficit)	8,783	5,650	1,170
Accumulated other comprehensive loss	(4,979)	(5,845)	(5,801)
Treasury stock, at cost	(251)	(341)	(313)
Total stockholders' equity	**15,293**	**11,105**	**6,582**
Total liabilities and stockholders' equity	**$ 75,372**	**$ 73,644**	**$ 72,288**

The assets are in order of those that are most liquid to those that are least liquid. Note that cash and cash equivalents are at the top, carried over from the statement of cash flows. Remember that current assets are those the company expects to use or convert to cash within 12 months. Notice that Delta specifically mentions its fuel inventory. That's a major asset for airlines that they "burn" through regularly. Noncurrent assets are more fixed and less liquid, like property and equipment.

Notice that Delta's total current assets have been falling year over year, but its total assets have been remaining relatively steady. If you look at the property and equipment line item, it seems as though Delta has been investing its liquid assets into new property and equipment, possibly new planes, software, etc.

One thing to realize about the balance sheet is that it doesn't always accurately reflect the true value of a company's assets. For instance, in the line item for property and equipment, you see "net of accumulated depreciation and amortization." Delta's airplanes show up on the balance sheet at their original purchase price that has been steadily depreciated down year over year. So a plane they bought 10 years ago for $100 million has had about half of its original cost depreciated, meaning it shows up on the balance sheet at $50 million. But Delta could probably sell that plane for much more than that amount. An even better example is real estate. Imagine Delta bought a property for its headquarters 30 years ago. By now, that property has been fully depreciated so it doesn't show up anywhere on the balance sheet, but it might be worth $80 million.

Like the listed assets, liabilities are in order of those that are due first to those that are due last. Current liabilities are those due in the next 12 months, like current debts and money owed to suppliers or vendors, and noncurrent liabilities are those due more than one year out, like long-term loans and employee pension payments. Notice that Delta lists loyalty program deferred revenue. This is the "money" in the form of airline tickets that Delta owes its customers for points they've earned but haven't used yet.

Overall, Delta's current liabilities have been climbing, which we partially explained with the loyalty program story. Their noncurrent liabilities are steadily falling, indicating that they're paying off debt. In fact, they're almost back to pre-pandemic levels.

Once we get through all assets and all liabilities, we can calculate total shareholders' or stockholders' equity, which is the difference between total assets and total liabilities. Delta's has been steadily climbing, pulling its equity ratio up and up to 20% in 2024.

The value of assets always equals liabilities plus equity, just like the value of a home equals the mortgage debt plus the equity the owner has in the home. So the last line of the balance sheet shows that balancing equation: total liabilities and shareholders' equity, which equals, or *balances* with, total assets.

What the Numbers Can Tell You About a Company

Delta is a great example of why understanding the balance sheet can help you understand the strength and value of a company, for what is probably an obvious reason: the dramatic fall-off in air travel in 2020 due to the pandemic, and then the surge in travel afterward.

For reference, here are the highlights of Delta's balance sheet and income statement for the key pandemic years, in millions:

| | December 31, | | | | | |
	2024	2023	2022	2021	2020	2019
Total current assets	9,844	10,269	13,011	15,940	17,404	8,249
Total assets	75,372	73,644	72,288	72,459	71,996	64,532
Total current liabilities	26,670	26,418	25,940	20,966	15,927	20,204
Total noncurrent liabilities	33,409	36,121	39,766	47,606	54,535	28,970
Total stockholders' equity	15,293	11,105	6,582	3,887	1,534	15,358

	December 31,					
	2024	2023	2022	2021	2020	2019
Total revenue	61,643	58,048	50,582	29,899	17,095	47,007
Total operating expenses	55,648	52,527	46,921	28,013	29,564	40,389
Operating income / (loss)	5,995	5,521	3,661	1,886	(12,469)	6,618
Net income / (loss)	3,457	4,609	1,318	280	(12,385)	4,767

Obviously, Delta took a huge hit in 2020, losing more than $12 billion. And its total stockholders' equity plummeted, too. But it still maintained positive total equity that year of more than $1.5 billion because it went into the pandemic with strong assets. And because of the strength of its balance sheet, it was able to borrow a substantial amount of money. Its long-term debts and financial obligations almost doubled because it had to take on loans to survive. But by the end of 2021, Delta had already paid off more than $2 billion of that debt and by 2024 had gotten their total non-current liabilities down to about $33 billion, reducing it by another $3 billion in 2024.

Delta's important ratios also took a hit during the pandemic, showing that it's important to look at these measures over time and in conjunction with the other drivers we've been discussing.

	2024	2023	2022	2021	2020	2019
Equity ratio (total stockholders' equity divided by total assets, as a percentage)	20.29%	15.08%	9.11%	5.36%	2.13%	23.8%
Current ratio (current asset divided by current liabilities)	.37	.39	.50	.76	1.09	.41
Return on assets (net income divided by total assets, as a percentage)	4.59%	6.26%	1.82%	0.39%	-17.20%	7.39%

But Delta leaders have been doing whatever they can to improve those ratios as fast as possible—like adjusting their loyalty program. Since 2020, they've been a bit of a mixed bag as Delta continues to try to reduce its debt burden while also investing in necessary assets for future growth—like cybersecurity assets.

> > >

While it might be a bit more difficult to see the connection between what you're selling and your customer's asset decisions, it all boils down to this: Your customer is investing in an asset every time they buy from you. The more you can communicate how that investment will help them earn a return—in language executives will respond to whenever they're the ultimate decision maker—the better.

›››››› *ASSETS IN REVIEW*

» A company's assets include everything it owns or controls, tangible or intangible, used to produce revenue, manage costs, and create profit, or that can be converted to cash. Leaders face the constant challenge of balancing asset strength and asset utilization to produce the maximum return on investment and to ensure future profitability.

» Asset strength or financial strength reflects the overall capability of a company to pay its bills, meet its financial obligations, overcome difficulties, take advantage of opportunities, and generate cash flow and profits even in economic downturns. Asset strength is assessed by looking at a company's

  · liquidity, or the amount of its cash, cash equivalents, and assets that could easily be turned into cash

  · equity, or the value of its assets minus its financial liabilities, like debts

  · ability to cover its financial obligations or pay its bills over the next 12 months

» Companies with great asset strength have better capability to move quickly to solve problems and take advantage of market opportunities.

» Asset utilization is the measure of how productively a company's assets are working to make money—to drive sales and profits. Asset utilization can be improved by eliminating inefficient or non-producing assets, getting more productivity from existing assets, making business process more efficient, and enabling employees to use their time more effectively.

» As a salesperson, you need to be familiar with an important measure that doesn't show up on any financial statement: return on investment (ROI). ROI is the return earned on or benefit gained from an investment divided by the cost of it and is shown as a percentage. Your primary role is to be able to show a good return on any investment in assets you're asking your customer to make.

» Thinking about all of the ways your offering can positively impact asset utilization is one way to boost the value or benefit in the minds of your customers.

» The important asset measures are:

  • Equity ratio: total stockholders' equity divided by total assets

  • Current ratio: current assets divided by current liabilities; a measure that helps you understand how well prepared a company is to cover its debts over the next 12 months

  • Return on assets: net income divided by total assets; a measure of how efficiently and productively a company uses its assets

  • Inventory turnover: cost of goods sold divided by the average value of inventory on hand; it's an asset utilization measure that is important in many industries but not all

» Information about assets can be found on the balance sheet, which is based on the equation: Asset − Liabilities = Equity. It lists short-term and long-term assets, short-term and long-term liabilities, and then shows total stockholders' equity, or all assets minus all liabilities.

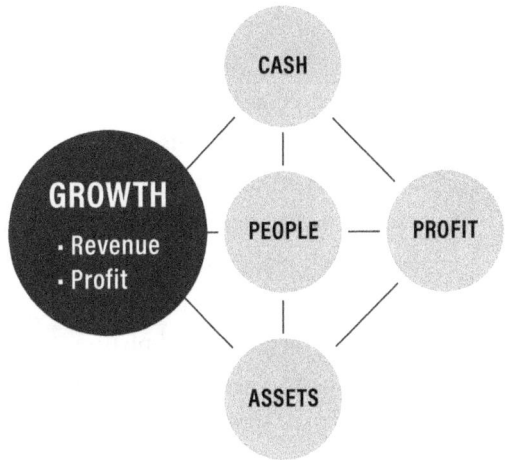

CHAPTER 5

GROWTH

"Even if you are on the right track, you'll get run over if you just sit there." —Tom Sims, American humorist (often misattributed to Will Rogers)

HAVE YOU EVER WORKED FOR A SUCCESSFUL, profitable, high-growth company? What was it like? Exciting, right? People were energized. They had new opportunities to be involved in interesting projects. Career paths opened up as the company expanded. Talented people joined the organization, offering stimulating perspectives and innovative ideas. Productivity increased, bonuses were handed out, and salaries were competitive. Morale was high. And as a salesperson, your job was just a little easier because you represented a company that was consistently improving and innovating its products and services.

But for a company that isn't adapting to changes in its environment by offering greater value, better prices, or innovative products, the picture is very different. Customers turn to competitors, the company begins losing market share, and the best people leave. Sales stall and then decrease; margins and profitability shrink; stock price drops and shareholders are disappointed; cost-cutting increases; people are let go; morale decreases; productivity, quality, and service fall; more customers turn to competitors and the company loses more market share; stock price drops further; sales decrease even more; profitability shrinks further...

Well, you get the sad picture.

These vastly different pictures explain why investors expect growth, employees are energized by it, customers are attracted to it, and executives are measured by it. They explain why growth might be any leader's—especially those in the C-suite—number one priority. Some small mom-and-pop operations can continue year after year at about the same level of sales and profitability, providing a nice livelihood for a small group of people, but any larger or publicly held enterprise that doesn't grow its sales and profits risks this "downward decline and die" cycle that ultimately spells doom—or at least a buy-out by a competitor. So sustainable, profitable growth is the primary objective of any CEO of a publicly held company who wants to keep his or her job!

A company measures its growth in many ways: increase in number of employees, market share, number of offices, number of regions served, number of customers, and so on. But generally, **when businesspeople are talking about growth and financials, they're talking about steadily increasing revenue, profit, and earnings per share.** But as a salesperson, what's most important for you to know is what *your* customer is trying to grow, how they're trying to accomplish that goal, and what you can do to help them. And as a sales professional, you *want* growth for your customers and clients—because the more they grow, the more opportunities you have to sell to them and contribute to your *own* company's growth. So let's look at what you can do to actively help them along the way.

For a perfect example, picture the box of the 12-pack of Coke or other soda cans that might be sitting in your refrigerator right now. The whole box fits neatly onto a shelf, and when you take a can from the front, the next one drops in to take its place. The 12-count fridge pack puts more Cokes in people's refrigerators—and more revenue in Coca-Cola's coffers. But Coca-Cola didn't create that growth-driver; its partner did.

Alcoa manufactures aluminum, including aluminum cans. In the 1990s, they brought some of their top engineers, designers, and marketers into a hotel conference room. In the middle of that conference room was a refrigerator. The job they gave their employees was to figure out the best way to get the maximum number of cans into the refrigerator while taking up the least amount of valuable space. They were trying to solve the problem of people putting only a few cans in at a time, which meant that when there were no cold cans, people chose something else to drink. They analyzed every possible configuration until they came up with what most of us are familiar with now—the 12-count fridge pack—maximizing the often-unused back of fridge space.

Alcoa's salespeople pitched the packaging idea to Coca-Cola. From Coke's own data, that one idea increased their revenue by roughly 10% in the first year—and also increased Alcoa's!

You're a conduit between your company and your customers. You carry ideas between the two that have the potential to help either of them grow. So let's look at how companies focus on growth so you can maximize your contribution and your value.

GROWTH TELLS YOU WHERE A COMPANY IS HEADED

Change is a constant in business, and growth tells you how well a company is adapting to it, which says a lot about its future. Whether it's new competition, evolving customer needs, or some other shift in the marketplace, when a company successfully pursues opportunities in a changing marketplace, it grows.

Leaders striving to find and take advantage of those opportunities have to take risks. They have to invest company assets to support a strategy they hope will produce more growth in the future. If they miscalculate or misjudge a growth opportunity, or if competitors undercut their prices and steal customers, or if the economy takes an unexpected downturn, they can find their costs increasing faster than sales. They can find that they need assets to respond to a new change, assets they don't have anymore. Developing strategies for growth and balancing the decisions to keep the company stable and pursue opportunities isn't easy. What makes all the difference is the skill of the leaders in establishing a vision for the company, creating sound strategy based on that vision, and then executing the strategy successfully.

Leaders pursue growth strategies in two areas: *organic growth* (internal growth strategies) and *inorganic growth* (growth through mergers, acquisitions, and possibly even partnerships). And a company's development stage can influence how much growth those strategies create.

Organic Growth

A business grows organically, from the inside, when it expands using internal resources, such as training new employees, opening new offices or stores, building new plants to produce more goods or serve different customers, broadening its marketing reach into new geographic or demographic areas, or developing and launching new products and services.

Organic growth offers maximum control over the timing of the expansion and the nature of the operations. There is generally less risk because management controls most aspects of the plan or strategy, and the company is usually expanding into business areas it already understands.

However, the business also incurs 100% of the costs of expansion and operation, which can be considerable. Organic growth can also be slow; it might take years for new sales territories to generate revenue, for new people to become fully trained and productive, for new plants to become profitable, and for new product lines and technologies to be developed. And growth strategies don't always play out as leaders expect. What if Coke had invested in the fridge pack—designing and manufacturing the new packaging, marketing it to consumers, selling it into retailers—and it hadn't produced an increase in the total number of cans sold? The company would have lost that invested cash and not earned any return.

Despite the potential risk of investing in new products, new regions, or new customer segments, the upside of potential growth outweighs the risk for the vast majority of companies.

Inorganic Growth

To grow revenue faster, companies often buy, or merge with, existing businesses. New customers and revenue streams are immediate. Management teams, employees, production plants, offices, salespeople, and other company assets are already in place. Product brands and distribution channels are already established. And if they're a competitor, the company doing the buying can boost market share and get access to innovative ideas and products. ExxonMobil, Microsoft, and United-Health Group are known for taking this approach.

But inorganic growth carries its own set of challenges. It takes a lot of capital to acquire another business—a big investment that can affect the balance sheet. And achieving two usual goals in mergers—reducing costs by combining operations and finding synergy in sales—is rarely seamless. Employees might be terminated, information and technology systems might be incompatible, and merging organizational cultures can raise unanticipated resistance. In fact, studies have shown that 50% to 85% of public company mergers and acquisitions don't meet the business objectives set by the leadership team. While some work out wonderfully, like the match between Disney and Pixar, others actually erode the value of the business, like the AOL Time Warner merger in 2000 that cost shareholders more than $200 billion.

The Stages of Development

When you're trying to understand a customer's growth story, one point of context is where the company is in its development journey. When investors or analysts talk about development or growth, they'll reference where a company is in the business lifecycle: start-up, growth, maturity, renewal/decline. This can be a useful way to think about how a company grows, but it's also misleading. First, having one stage labeled "growth" implies that the company isn't growing the rest of the time. Of course it is—until it's declining. Second, while we use the term *life cycle*, businesses rarely progress from one stage to another in a step-by-step fashion. A company might move back and forth between growth and maturity as new markets or technologies become available. Or a new division within a mature company might exhibit all of the behaviors of a startup.

That said, considering the stages of the life cycle can help you anticipate what type of growth you might expect in a client company. For instance, a start-up might struggle along for a while with little growth, but then hit its stride and take off. This is the growth stage, and it can move a company from a small operation to a global organization. And while fast growth can be a wonderful thing, it can often require risky investments. Lots of companies never make it past the start-up stage, and many don't make it to maturity. Those that do typically see a slower growth rate, but that doesn't mean the company is unhealthy. It's just a lot easier to grow from $400,000 to $600,000 in one year, a 50% growth rate, than it is to grow from $40 billion to $60 billion.

> > >

As a salesperson, depending on the products or services you're selling, you might be able to help your clients improve their organic growth or make their inorganic growth more successful. If your offering supports any kind of growth strategy, be as clear as you can about the possible benefits.

TRACKING GROWTH IN KEY NUMBERS

By what percentage did company revenue—the top line on the income statement—grow this year compared to last, or this quarter compared to the same quarter last year? By what percentage did company profits—the bottom line—grow this period compared to last? The *rate* of growth, or percentage increase between one period and the next, of both revenue and profit are widely used criteria for evaluating the stock price and worth of any company. When analysts say that a company is growing by a certain percentage, they usually mean its revenue is growing—year-over-year or quarter-over-quarter—by that percentage.

Of course, what we hope to see is growth in both the top line and the bottom line. That's a good indicator that the growth is sustainable and that the company is less likely to suddenly crash and burn. Ideally, in a mature company, we would like to see profits growing at a faster rate than revenues, because it indicates the company is gaining efficiencies and economies of scale. That said, declining profits in the short term may not be an issue, if the company shows it's reinvesting its income to grow even more in the future.

Increase in earnings per share (EPS) is another critical measure of growth for a mature *public* company. Earnings per share refers to the profits generated per share of common stock outstanding, and the more profit generated, the more valuable the company is. Earnings per share are calculated by dividing the net income by the average number of shares of common stock outstanding; ideally, EPS will increase period over period.

Finally, don't ignore trends in cash flow from operations, an important indicator of how efficiently and successfully a company is operating its core business, and stock price, a number that leaders are always concerned about. Investors or shareholders respond to the future with real intensity, and if the future isn't looking better than the past, they'll take their money and go elsewhere. You can play a role in driving growth momentum and optimism.

CALCULATING GROWTH

You might calculate growth often—when trying to analyze how much more revenue you've brought in over the last few years for your company—but let's run through a quick review.

$$\frac{\text{New number} - \text{Previous number}}{\text{Previous number}} \times 100 = \text{Growth Rate (Percent)}$$

We brought up Coca-Cola earlier, so let's use them as an example. Using their income statement for 2024, we can calculate that revenue grew 2.9% and net income fell 0.8%.

$$\frac{\$47{,}061{,}000{,}000 - \$45{,}754{,}000{,}000}{\$45{,}754{,}000{,}000} \times 100 = 2.9\% \text{ Revenue Growth}$$

$$\frac{\$10{,}631{,}000{,}000 - \$10{,}714{,}000{,}000}{\$10{,}714{,}000{,}000} \times 100 = -1\% \text{ Net Income Growth}$$

Understanding Your Clients' Growth

Like all numbers we've covered in this book, growth measures have to be explored together. It's especially important to look at the bottom-line profit growth alongside the top-line revenue growth. In our courses, we often boil it down to this: If you have only one minute to prepare for a meeting, look at revenue and profit. If revenue has grown but profit hasn't, costs are increasing somewhere and your client is going to be focused on reducing them. If you see the opposite—profits are up but revenue is flat or down—your client is going to be focused on growing revenue by increasing customers, number of products sold, prices, and other strategies. Just that bit of data can tell you how to approach a conversation.

If revenue and profits are both growing, don't immediately take it as a sign that there aren't any hurdles to tackle. If profits are growing at a slower *rate*, the company's costs are rising faster than its revenue, reducing its profit *margin* even if its actual profit *dollars* are increasing. Leaders are going to have a close eye on that, especially if profit margin has been on a downward trend over time.

Revenue and profit matter, but what matters most is understanding how *your* client currently thinks about growth. If you were selling to Coca-Cola, for instance, and did a little research, you would quickly discover that they're very transparent about their long-term growth targets. In addition to a cash flow ratio goal, they list the following in most of their investor presentations:

- Organic revenue growth of 4% to 6%.
- Operating income growth of 6% to 8%.
- EPS growth of 7% to 9%.

From 2021 to 2022, Coke's revenue was increasing but its profit, and therefore its EPS, was declining. Then they returned to top- and bottom-line growth in 2023. That's an anomaly worth looking into.

In 2022, cost of goods sold increased by about $2.7 billion and "other operating charges" increased by almost $400 million. Overall, operating income did increase, a good sign, but at a rate of about 6% rather than the 11% increase in revenue. Again, why? The next step is to turn to the company's press release about its annual statements. One sentence in it tells us a lot: "For both the quarter and the full year, operating margin benefited from strong topline growth but was *unfavorably impacted* by the BODYARMOR acquisition, higher operating costs, an increase in marketing investments versus the prior year."

Coca-Cola Company Consolidated Statement of Income

(In millions except per share data)

	Years Ended December 31			
	2024	2023	2022	2021
Net Operating Revenues	$ 47,061	$ 45,754	$ 43,004	$ 38,655
Cost of goods sold	18,324	18,520	18,000	15,357
Gross Profit	28,737	27,234	25,004	23,298
Selling, general, and administrative expenses	14,582	13,972	12,880	12,144
Other operating charges	4,163	1,951	1,215	846
Operating Income	9,992	11,311	10,909	10,308
Interest income	988	907	449	276
Interest expense	1,656	1,527	882	1,597
Equity income (loss) – net	1,770	1,691	1,472	1,438
Other income (loss) – net	1,992	570	(262)	2,000
Income Before Income Taxes	13,086	12,952	11,686	12,425
Income taxes	2,437	2,249	2,115	2,621
Consolidated Net Income	10,649	10,703	9,571	9,804
Less: Net income (loss) attributable to noncontrolling interests	18	(11)	29	33
Net Income Attributable to Owners of the Coca-Cola Company	$ 10,631	$ 10,714	$ 9,542	$ 9,771
Basic net income per share	2.47	2.48	2.20	2.26
Diluted net income per share	2.46	2.47	2.19	2.25

Coke had pursued an inorganic growth strategy—acquiring BODYARMOR, a sports drink company—and it hadn't fully paid off by the end of 2022. Inflation and supply chain issues were also problematic in 2022, making it hard to contain operating costs. And they had pursued an organic growth strategy—increasing investments in marketing—which increased costs.

Despite the expected headwinds from the BODYARMOR acquisition, in 2023, Coke was able to reverse the profit trend and surpass some of their growth targets. But they faced headwinds again in 2024 in part because of the challenges of the BODYARMOR acquisition.

Once you know what your customers are trying to grow and have calculated whether growth is happening for them or not, the big question is: How will you use what you learn to align your solution with your customers' growth goals?

LEVERAGING GROWTH IN THE SALES PROCESS

Even if your customer isn't broadcasting their growth goals to the world, they still want it. And you can always find a way to leverage it.

Not long ago, we received an email from a patient-monitoring device salesperson—a clinically trained nurse with 15 years of experience and no business background. She knew the products of her company, Philips Healthcare, inside and out and had successfully sold devices to nurses, physicians, and department heads for years. But given the state of the healthcare industry and the challenge hospitals have been having for years with rising costs and falling profits, she was increasingly running into struggles.

After learning about the importance of profitability and growth, she started thinking about her customers' needs differently. When she learned that one of her customers was struggling with readmission rates, she recognized an opportunity to help. Under the Affordable Care Act, a hospital can't be reimbursed if a patient is re-admitted for the same condition within 30 days. Some Philips solutions have algorithms built in that can detect and prevent many of the things that lead to re-admission.

In the past, this salesperson, with her nursing background, had sold the features as a benefit for patients and often overworked nurses. She decided to approach the chief nursing officer instead. She explained how Philips Healthcare solutions could save the hospital 30% on readmission costs and help them grow their bottom line. She won the deal.

Growth strategies often come from within an organization—from sales and marketing teams' direct influence to people in support functions who find ways to optimize processes and increase margins. But sometimes, the most powerful growth strategies come from third parties— from partner organizations or even from sales professionals like you.

Regardless, what's crucial is to **understand and align your products**

and services with the growth strategies your customer is trying to execute. If growth is their biggest priority, it should be your biggest priority in terms of your research and analysis. Start with the numbers, and then consider these questions:

- How, in general, does your product or service help customers grow?

- Do you know the growth strategies of your most important customers—their plans for improving their numbers? Are they organic or inorganic or both?

- Do you know their biggest obstacles to growth or what hurdles they're facing as they try to execute their strategies?

- Have you had a growth discussion with your contacts?

- Have any of your customers used your product or service in a unique or creative way that helped them grow?

- How, specifically, can your product or service help your most important clients grow?

Spend just a few minutes reading what the company has to say about the numbers (as we did in the Coca-Cola example), ask your contacts for more information if you need it, and then show how valuable you can be to their future growth.

› › › › › *GROWTH IN REVIEW*

» Companies—yours and your customers'—either continue to grow or risk dying. Companies growing revenue and profit tend to be more energized, be more innovative in their products and services, expand their market share, and attract motivated top talent. Companies not growing can enter a "downward decline and die" cycle of higher costs, lower sales, lost market share, lower share price, cost cutting, reduction in workforce, demoralized employees, lost customers, more loss of market share, and so on. Every leader's top priority is to ensure sustainable growth in order to create value for owners or shareholders, especially in publicly traded companies.

» Companies use organic growth strategies and inorganic growth strategies. Organic means internal investment and expansion. Inorganic means merging with or acquiring new businesses to increase revenue, profits, and cash flow.

» Both top-line revenue growth and bottom-line income or profit growth are essential over time, which means growth is reflected primarily on a company's income statement. The investment community mainly looks at the revenue and income growth of a company and especially growth in earnings per share when valuing its stock. Over time, and especially in mature companies, you want to see a higher growth *rate* for profit than revenue.

» When approaching a conversation, consider this: If revenue is up but profit isn't, costs are increasing somewhere and your client is going to be focused on reducing them. If profits are up but revenue is flat or down, your client is going to be focused on increasing customers, the number of products sold, and other revenue strategies.

» As a salesperson, it's crucial to understand and align your products and services with the growth strategies your customer is trying to execute. Or, put another way, help them overcome their growth obstacles. Can you help them be more innovative? Can you help them move into a new market? Can you help them work through a merger or acquisition more successfully and efficiently? Anything you can do to positively influence their growth rate will make you a valuable partner.

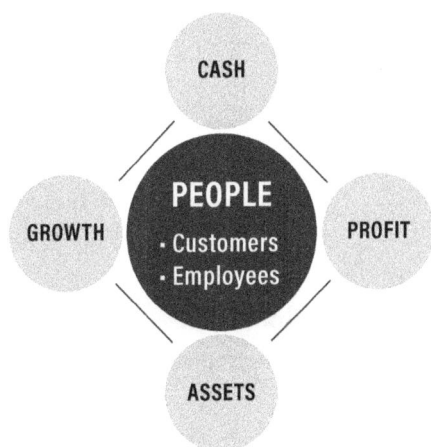

CASH

PEOPLE
· Customers
· Employees

GROWTH

PROFIT

ASSETS

CHAPTER 6

PEOPLE

"You don't build a business.
You build people, and people build the business."
—Zig Ziglar

HUGO WAS A SALESPERSON FOR AN ONLINE recruitment and hiring platform that offered large-scale solutions for big businesses. He had been selling other product lines to smaller and mid-sized businesses and knew exactly how to help HR professionals. Now, he would be selling to a cross-functional group of senior leaders who needed the sophisticated data and analytics tools his company offered.

Hugo understood the tools and how to use them. Being a bit of a data geek, he could talk all about the different ways to look at segments of data or create comparisons across departments and divisions. But he was struggling to get the leaders he met with excited about any of that.

After learning more about how employees drive a business and the common challenges and concerns they face, Hugo tried a different approach. Before his next meeting, he read a couple of articles about the big employee challenges in his customer's industry. Then, he skimmed the company's most recent annual report to find out what the CEO had said about talent recruiting and retention challenges. In less than 10 minutes, Hugo learned two vital pieces of information. First, the biggest challenge in the industry overall was a lack of skilled workers, especially in the US. And second, the CEO felt the company's biggest employee challenge was low engagement and how it added to rising recruitment costs.

Well prepared, Hugo addressed these issues early in the meeting, and everybody perked up. He described how the analytics tools could be fine-tuned to improve engagement by identifying employees who would not only have the necessary skills but also fit into the company culture. He also shared the broader talent market intelligence his company offered, which would allow the company to identify talent and skills hotspots across the country to target their recruiting efforts, helping them make faster and better employment decisions. They signed on the next week for a three-month trial period.

In our graphic model of the 5 Business Drivers, **we place people in the middle because people make the decisions, supply the financial resources, buy the products, provide the labor and services, and otherwise create and contribute to everything else about a business.** They drive cash, profit, assets, and growth—and great people strategies are the most sustainable way to positively impact those drivers. Too many companies get the order reversed.

You are a person who contributes directly to the cash, profit, assets, and growth of your company! And think about some of the stories we've told in the previous chapters. Who came up with the idea for Delta to change how it pushed planes back from the terminal, saving the company time and money? Who developed the fridge pack that Coca-Cola used to dramatically increase revenue by better meeting the needs of their customers? Who delivers every UPS package? People. People. People.

If a business wants to be successful, it needs to meet and exceed— or even better, *anticipate*—the wants, needs, and expectations of employees, customers, and other important stakeholders. For publicly traded companies, that includes shareholders, too.

You don't have to be selling human resource tools to consider the people driver in your customer's business. When you understand your customer's strategies and challenges as they relate to employees, customers, and shareholders, your conversations will be more nuanced, more targeted, and more effective—because these people influence all other drivers. So let's look at the three most important groups for any business and what we can learn from them.

EMPLOYEES: CULTURE, ENGAGEMENT, COLLABORATION

Peter Drucker, the renowned management expert, once wrote, "Culture eats strategy for breakfast." No strategy, no matter how ingenious, can survive a lousy culture that leaves employees feeling dissatisfied, disrespected, and underappreciated. When the people who are responsible for critical business operations feel like that, how invested are they going to be in the success of their team or company?

A business's number-one resource is its employees. Their productivity and the effectiveness of their decision making will always be key drivers of a company's success.

The most successful companies have the best employees with the longest tenures. They're not wasting money on unnecessary turnover, which can cost from $5,000 for a minimum wage position to 200% of annual salary for a leadership position. In these companies, a strong, positive, employee-focused culture helps ensure that employees have strong relationships with management, benefits and perks that are meaningful to them, and a working environment that keeps them engaged and satisfied. Companies that skip out on these efforts pay a steep price. According to Gallup estimates, "low employee engagement costs the global economy US$8.9 trillion"—per year.[11]

With the stakes this high, every company, no matter how much pressure it's facing from shareholders, can and should use its resources to create an engaging culture that attracts top talent and keeps productivity high. Study after study has shown that the primary reasons companies lose their valuable, talented employees all relate to culture issues, like poor management habits, lack of development opportunities, and employees' lack of clarity about how they make a difference in the organization by impacting business results. In our courses, we always say that people will work hard for a paycheck, harder for a person, and hardest for a purpose. Creating a compelling culture takes an understanding of the value of people and a commitment to developing a great working environment.

We know leaders care about this issue. In a recent survey, when CEOs were asked about their biggest concerns, the top three were all about people—specifically "attracting and retaining top talent," "developing the next generation of leaders," and "maintaining an engaged workforce."[12] The challenge is devoting the resources necessary to make these goals a reality. It can be easy to make commitments when times are good, but when the tide turns, giving into the temptation to cut costs and "do more with less" can damage the culture and risks burning people out. Productive and profitable companies are usually committed to ongoing employee and culture development—in good times and bad.

For example, at the Ritz-Carlton (a division of Marriott International), employee education and training is key to the company's fabled success in guest satisfaction. The company conducts detailed analyses of all aspects of its operations, involving employees at every level. Ritz-Carlton has identified 97 potential problems that may arrive with overnight guests, and first-year managers and employees receive more than 250 hours of training on how to handle these issues. Not only do these practices keep the customers happy, but Ritz-Carlton also enjoys the lowest turnover rate of any luxury hotel chain in the industry.

T-Mobile also has a strong focus on employees, especially given that many of its team members are retail workers in their almost 7,000 stores across the US. Their focus on people overall has helped them grow their revenue fourfold, from about $20 billion to almost $80 billion, over the last 10 years. The company is known for offering the same level of benefits to every permanent employee throughout the company, both full-time and part-time. They're also devoted to employing service members and their spouses, recognizing how hard it can be to build a career when your spouse's job requires you to move every few years. Here's what T-Mobile shares at the top of the "People" page of their website.

> Our success begins and ends with our employees.
>
> Investing in our people is a top priority. We offer everyone on Team Magenta opportunities to learn, grow, recharge, and thrive throughout their career. We've built an open and encouraging workplace with the tools and resources that empower our people to do their best work. Our people make us the unstoppable Un-carrier.

And they back up the good talk with transparent data about their investments in employees in their annual corporate responsibility report. Given the size of the company and the spread of employees across the US, its Glassdoor rating is solid at 3.7.

So what does culture have to do with the sales process? Well, you're selling into that culture, and its nuances can influence how your product or service might be implemented, what hurdles you might face during the sales process or trial phases, and how you might position your solution depending on who you're talking to in the organization. In Part 2, we'll share a resource to help you consider the specific focus or concerns of the people you meet with—all of whom are employees—during the sales process so you can align with them, but the culture can influence how your conversations play out. If the culture is strong and positive, you can leverage it. If it's in trouble—if people are leaving or engagement is low—you can consider opportunities to help.

Of course, beyond culture issues, you might be able to help your prospects improve overall productivity and decision making—as Hugo from the start of the chapter was doing. Yes, he was helping them improve their talent acquisition, but he was also helping them make that process more efficient, reducing the people hours spent on each hire through better intelligence.

Remember, while culture, engagement, and productivity are universal concerns, how those play out from company to company and industry to industry can be quite different.

CUSTOMERS: THE LIFEBLOOD OF ANY BUSINESS

"We've said it for years, investing in customers leads to customer growth, which leads to revenue growth, which if we run the company well leads to EBITDA and cash flow growth, which we invest right back into our customers and their network experience, which is what started the success cycle in the first place."[13] This quote from Mike Sievert, CEO of T-Mobile, captures perfectly how paying attention to customers can improve performance on all the other drivers.

As a sales professional, you understand the deep value of happy customers at a personal level. You know they're the source of revenue and profit. You know that as essential and important as employees are in your business, they are there to serve the customers—the people who pay for your products and services, keeping your business alive.

Without customers, a company is quickly out of business. And every time you lose an existing customer, it costs the company. Depending upon your industry, the cost of getting a new customer is *two to ten times* more than the cost of keeping an existing customer, so you really want to keep the ones you have.

Ritz-Carlton, whose employee training policy we described, regularly ranks among the highest luxury hotel chains in the annual hotel-guest-satisfaction survey conducted by J.D. Power and Associates. It has ranked number one in this category almost every year since 2007, only occasionally slipping into second place. It's also the only two-time winner of the Malcolm Baldrige National Quality Award in the service category. Throughout this luxury hotel chain, one strategic goal is 100% customer retention. Every employee is empowered to spend up to $2,000—without checking with anyone, using only his or her best judgment—to immediately correct any problem or handle any guest complaint.

But to avoid having to pay to correct too many problems, Ritz-Carlton proactively performs regular and meaningful customer reviews to assess how well it is satisfying its customers' needs and expectations. This is something that most companies do, something your own company probably does, and it's important to understand your role in improving customer satisfaction, especially as one of the first people customers interact with. You can start by answering the following four questions:

- Who is your most important customer right now?
- What specifically do they want from you?
- How would your customer rate you on how well you're meeting their needs or expectations?
- What could you do differently to improve?

The next section might give you some ideas for coming up with stronger answers to these questions.

Go Deeper, Anticipate, and Innovate

It's likely you've heard this favorite Henry Ford adage on innovation: "If I had asked people what they wanted, they would have said faster horses." Whether Ford really said that or not is up for debate, but the spirit is certainly true. Customers often don't recognize their own needs or how best to meet them, and they don't recognize the possibilities beyond what they think or expect in the moment. Keeping current customers and attracting new ones means understanding and fulfilling needs they might never articulate. That's why the most successful companies go deeper than the immediate or obvious, work to anticipate future needs, and innovate to fulfill them.

Anyone in sales (and marketing) knows that it's absolutely necessary to understand what your customer is really buying from you—beyond the obvious. When families eat out, are parents buying hamburgers or are they buying a fun night out with the kids and a break from the grind of cooking dinner? Customers buy automobiles not just for transportation but also for status and prestige. They buy clothing to make personal statements.

So why do customers buy your products and services? What do they really want or need? More than likely, they're paying for convenience, reliability, value, prestige, time savings, and other intangible benefits that are outgrowths of your product's actual use or application. And when you're selling business to business, your customers are fundamentally buying improved business performance, which is the whole reason we've written this book!

The long-term challenge for companies is that customers can't always identify what they'll want in the future, but leaders still have to plan for it. This makes effective anticipation, prediction, and innovation the ultimate competitive advantage. Innovative entrepreneurs—regardless of the size or maturity of their company—lead the consumer marketplace. Pocket-sized cell phones, GPS navigation, e-books, tablet computers, virtual reality devices, and AI-driven *everything* are just a few examples of game-changing product innovations, most of which we didn't know we needed. And the corporate graveyard is full of companies that failed to anticipate and innovate: Blockbuster, Borders, Yahoo, Blackberry, Toys "R" Us, and more.

How can you help clients anticipate market changes and maintain their competitive advantages? One strategy is to hold a regularly scheduled meeting with your key customers to stay up to date on their business, their roadmap, and any changes or challenges they may be facing.

Don't wait for a problem to arise before sitting down together—rather, keep your finger on the pulse of your key clients' day-to-day so you can anticipate their needs and support their growth and innovation.

The Ritz-Carlton is well-versed in anticipating customer needs, too. The company has a deliberate program of data capture and analysis, and they use this information to anticipate the needs of returning guests. From desired room temperature, to type and firmness of pillow and mattress, to preferred morning newspaper, fulfilling guest needs is the focus of not only the current stay, but every future stay.

Meeting the Needs of Your Customer's Customer

Lots of sales strategies and models help you better understand and meet the needs of your customer, but what many leave out of the equation is the next important step: meeting the needs of your *customer's customer*. If customers are the source of a business's financial success, anything you can do to improve your client's ability to serve its customers will make you a rockstar. Remember the story of Alcoa and Coca-Cola? Alcoa understood the behavior of Coca-Cola's customers in a way that allowed them to help Coke better meet their needs.

Your customers may also have "internal customers" they're supporting with your products or services. Internal customers are the people we all work with or serve *within* our organizations. If you can help your client contacts and decision makers serve their internal customers better—for example, make their bosses' lives easier—then your offerings become instrumental in the value they bring to their teams. And remember, *you* have internal customers, too, and you need to have a good understanding of their needs and expectations as well. Consider scheduling a regular meeting with your boss to discuss your performance and their perspective on the direction of sales initiatives and the company as a whole.

Take the time to consider the following questions for your most important prospects and customers, both external and internal:

- Who are my customer's external customers? What do they look like?

- Who are my customer's key internal customers? How does my customer support these people?

- How does my customer market and sell to their customers?

- How do customers engage with my customer after a sale? What does the customer service process look like? Is my customer known for its customer service?

SHAREHOLDERS: POWERFUL INFLUENCERS FOR PUBLIC COMPANIES

In Chapter 2, we told you about Apple's amazing stockpile of cash and other fairly liquid investments—and the shareholder lawsuit that forced Apple to distribute their excess cash to investors.

Since shareholders hold significant sway, savvy companies work hard to keep them happy. So, how do leaders know if they're doing that effectively? One quick and easy way is to look at the stock price. Is it going up or down?

The desire to keep shareholders happy—and keep the stock price rising—can put pressure on a business. It plays a powerful role in how corporate leaders make decisions, especially at the C-suite level. Public companies have to report their financial results every quarter, and leaders want them to seem impressive *every* quarter. Sometimes, to do that, they'll make choices that improve performance in the short term but hurt the company in the long term. For instance, they might lay off employees to boost the bottom line before they publish their next quarterly earnings statement. But in the process, they lose talent they need to innovate and grow in the long term, and they damage morale and engagement, which could impact the quality of their products and services in the near term. There's even a phrase for this kind of decision making: short-termism. The consulting giant McKinsey & Company conducted an intensive data-driven study of the issue and confirmed "that companies on the long-term end of the spectrum dramatically outperform those classified as short term."[14]

And investors and analysts are getting wise to this challenge. Sometimes, quarterly results might look great, but the stock price will fall—or the reverse. Shareholder optimism is driven by what they believe will happen in the future. You can help your own company *and* your customers build a strong foundation and be more innovative to help boost optimism.

Despite the risks of quarterly performance pressure, shareholders play a vital role: they give the company the cash, or capital, it needs to invest in growth. Without shareholders' investments, almost none of the big companies we all rely on today would exist. The best leaders balance the needs and expectations of investors with their ability to meet the needs and expectations of all other stakeholders and pursue growth over time.

As a salesperson, it's important to understand the short-term performance pressure public companies face, and the fact that they're constantly balancing that pressure against strategies for developing their customer and employee relationships for long-term success.

Most employees—especially those in management, where your buyers likely are—keep an eye on stock price, so it can be an effective talking point in a sales conversation. Before a call with a client, take a few minutes to review their company's stock prices over the last year and identify the causes of any big changes. Identifying ways your offerings can support a comeback or increase upward momentum could give you an advantage in closing a deal.

WHERE TO FIND CLUES ABOUT PEOPLE STRATEGIES AND CHALLENGES

Gathering information about people issues isn't quite as straightforward as assessing profit or revenue, but for larger and public companies, it doesn't take much effort to uncover important clues. Some questions you might try to answer because they could influence your next sales meeting include:

- Has the company recently laid off thousands of people or is it hiring like crazy?
- Is it on a Best Places to Work list?
- Has it recently broken ties with its biggest customer, and what might that mean about how it plans to achieve its goals?
- Is it expanding into a new customer segment?
- Are its employees threatening to go on strike?

You can find answers pretty quickly from a few sources of information.

- The **prepared remarks from the CEO during the last quarterly earnings call and the CEO's letter to shareholders** are both vital sources of information about people challenges and strategies and will likely address culture, talent acquisition, and customer opportunities. Much more on this in Resource 1.

- **The company's website:** What does it say about values, culture, and the employee and customer experience?

- **Glassdoor and similar sites:** Look at manager and employee ratings of the company, or even ratings by different groups of employees. But keep in mind that ratings can vary by industry and company size, so try to find a like-to-like comparison for reference. For instance, a public corporation like T-Mobile can't compete with a private partnership like Bain & Company, which has a 4.9 rating. T-Mobile has four times the number of employees doing much more varied work across far more locations.

- **News sites:** You can also do a quick search online for any headlines related to big people issues.

Target your research to the types of challenges your solution is best suited to help them solve. As you're gathering the info, consider this question: Which of the three stakeholder groups—employees, customers, or shareholders—seems to be of greatest importance right now?

> > >

The expectations of different groups of people in any company can sometimes appear to conflict, and strategies to keep everybody satisfied can converge in helpful or unhelpful ways. As we've illustrated, a hyperfocus on the shareholder can have a negative impact on employees, if not managed well. On the other hand, a hyper-focus on solving problems for customers can impact financial results negatively, at least in the short run, making shareholders unhappy. As a salesperson, anything you can do to help a company better fulfill the needs and wants of all three groups will put you in a strong, value-adding position.

> > > > > PEOPLE IN REVIEW

» People are the most important resource for any company. Employees, customers, and shareholders are the three important stakeholders.

» Successful companies usually have a history of strong employee satisfaction and longer employee tenure, so companies work hard to keep employees satisfied and attract top talent.

» Your customers are the lifeblood of your business. Customer satisfaction and loyalty are more a result of expectations met than actual results achieved. Delivering on customer expectations is critical in creating loyalty. Customers also buy more than just products. They purchase trustworthiness, convenience, prestige, or a memorable experience.

» Anticipating and innovating to meet unstated present and future customer needs is also key to long-term competitive success. It's how most breakthrough products and services are developed.

» Get to know your customers' customers. Understand their relationship, how they serve them, and what challenges they face to offer even more value.

» Set up regular meetings with your most important customers—including your own internal customers, like your boss—in order to stay up to date on their needs, perspectives, and challenges.

» Shareholder opinions about the future growth and value of a company have a big impact on a company's stock price. If leaders aren't careful, the desire to impress shareholders every quarter can lead to short-term decision making that undercuts the success of the company long term.

» To learn as much as possible about your customers' people challenges, turn to the annual report and the CEO's letter to shareholders, employee review sites like Glassdoor, and general news sites.

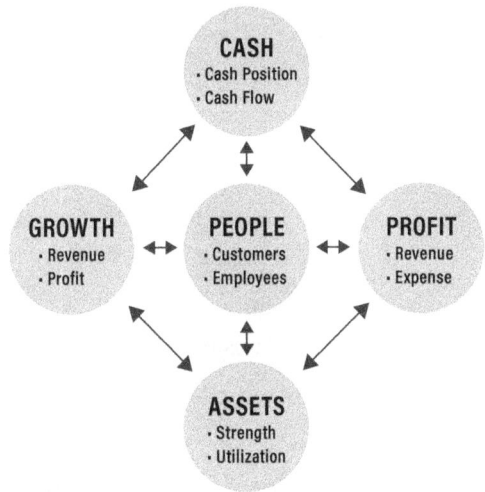

CHAPTER 7

THE BIG PICTURE: LINKING THE 5 BUSINESS DRIVERS

"The whole is more than the sum of its parts." —Aristotle

FOR SIX DECADES, TOYOTA GENERATED PROFITS YEAR after year. Then in 2009, its record crumbled under the pressure of the global recession and it booked its first annual net loss—of $7.7 billion. And the recession was just the first in a string of bad news for Toyota. There was a massive recall in 2009 and 2010 to solve an accelerator problem, which some claim was the result of an overdeveloped focus on controlling costs. Next came a fine of almost $16 million from the U.S. government for not alerting officials to the problem early enough. And then, a horrific earthquake hit Japan in March 2011, causing heartbreak and devastation for Toyota's home country and an ongoing loss of production as suppliers were unable to fill orders.

Despite the hits that kept coming, Toyota focused on what it knew best: making cars people wanted as efficiently as possible. It declared a state of profit emergency in 2009 and took drastic measures to book a profit in 2010. The plan?

- Deliver more eco-friendly vehicles, or more hybrid models, and piggyback on government tax breaks.

- Introduce special editions to meet the specific needs of consumers in certain regions.

- Cut variable costs by about $3.5 billion by reducing costs at manufacturing plants, among other strategies.

- Cut overhead costs by about $4.75 billion by reducing capital expenditures. The company closed and sold a major plant, for instance.

- Reduce R&D expenses by streamlining product development.

- Reduce general and administrative costs, such as travel expenses.

- Improve labor efficiency by implementing job sharing and other measures.

Did it work? Absolutely. Despite the continued global economic crisis, the company earned $2.2 billion in 2010.

Toyota has excelled in ways that helped it weather a violent storm. What are the keys to the company's success? Asset strength, a clear vision of what consumers want now and in the future, consistent revenue growth, and efficient asset utilization and operations to generate profits and cash. In short, the company understood each of the 5 Drivers: cash, profit, assets, growth, and people. If Toyota had not been so strong across all five, it would never have been able to achieve this one-year turnaround in profit, which set it up to earn more than $19 billion in 2016 and more than $33 billion in 2024.

This is an older story, but a great one for illustrating how the 5 Drivers feed each other. A company that excels in any one driver typically excels in others—and frequently, in all of them. The 5 Drivers, as we've seen in the previous five chapters, are interdependent; any change in one driver affects the others, and over the long term, it's impossible to be excellent in one and severely deficient in the others.

You can see this play out in the three core financial statements we've covered, which are interdependent just like the drivers. The income statement begins with revenues and ends with net income. Net income is the first line on the statement of cash flows, which then shows cash flowing into and out of the company to end with a calculation of the current amount of cash and cash equivalents. The balance sheet then begins with cash and cash equivalents and outlines other assets and liabilities to get to a calculation of shareholder's equity. The three statements start with a reflection of the activities the firm engages in with customers (revenues) and then illustrate how those activities drive greater value for shareholders (shareholder's equity). The graphic here shows the connections, using sample numbers.

Financial Statements: Interrelationship

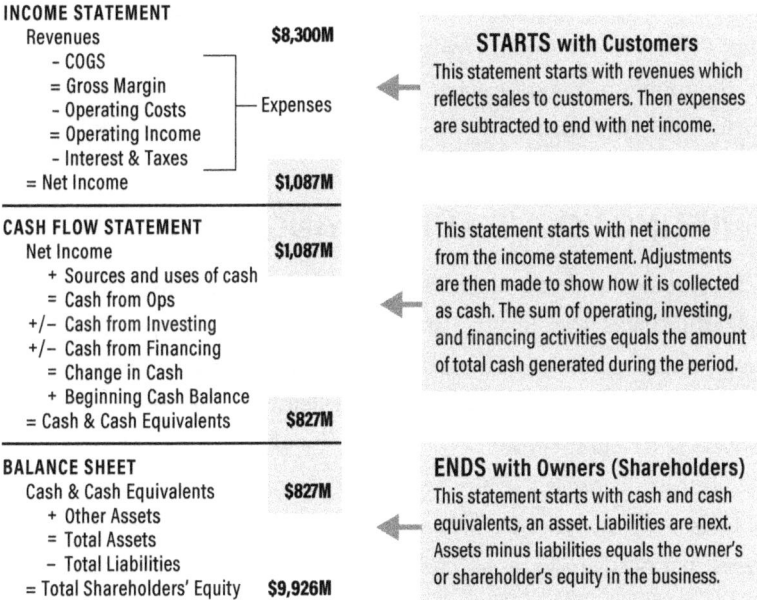

INCOME STATEMENT

Revenues	$8,300M
- COGS	
= Gross Margin	
- Operating Costs	Expenses
= Operating Income	
- Interest & Taxes	
= Net Income	$1,087M

STARTS with Customers
This statement starts with revenues which reflects sales to customers. Then expenses are subtracted to end with net income.

CASH FLOW STATEMENT

Net Income	$1,087M
+ Sources and uses of cash	
= Cash from Ops	
+/- Cash from Investing	
+/- Cash from Financing	
= Change in Cash	
+ Beginning Cash Balance	
= Cash & Cash Equivalents	$827M

This statement starts with net income from the income statement. Adjustments are then made to show how it is collected as cash. The sum of operating, investing, and financing activities equals the amount of total cash generated during the period.

BALANCE SHEET

Cash & Cash Equivalents	$827M
+ Other Assets	
= Total Assets	
- Total Liabilities	
= Total Shareholders' Equity	$9,926M

ENDS with Owners (Shareholders)
This statement starts with cash and cash equivalents, an asset. Liabilities are next. Assets minus liabilities equals the owner's or shareholder's equity in the business.

In our courses, we always point out that people are present all the way through the statements and how they are linked together: We start with customers at the top, in the form of revenue, and end with shareholder's equity. And employees make everything in between possible, doing the work of translating value to customers into value to owners or shareholders.

Trying to track all the drivers and consider how to influence or leverage them might seem a little overwhelming—after all, there are a lot of moving parts to keep track of. It's like a CEO has five plates on five sticks. They're trying to make sure each one is level and spinning fast. If they get overly focused on one plate for too long, say profit, other plates might start to wobble, like people and assets. In the short-term, their focus will shift to whichever driver seems to need attention, but long term they need to be attentive to all the plates.

We've given you the foundation to recognize this challenge and spot opportunities to help your customers' keep all their plates spinning, achieving their goals for each driver. And in Part 2, we're going to give you tools to pull it all together for specific clients. For now, all that's left is to try to anticipate what a customer's priorities might be in the moment based on what you know about the company and the business environment.

SHIFTING FOCUS AND STAYING INFORMED

CEOs, senior leaders and managers, and the company as a whole naturally shift focus from one driver to another over time. Depending on the stage of an organization's development and other internal, external, and historical factors, senior management might give priority to different drivers at different times.

But just because a company prioritizes one driver doesn't mean that it loses sight of the other four—or at least it shouldn't. A company in crisis that needs to focus on cash, for instance, shouldn't ignore its customers or forget about long-term growth. In fact, a renewed customer focus might be the key to generating the cash required to get out of trouble in the short term and fuel growth in the long term.

Generally, though, you can expect a CEO to prioritize certain drivers based on the company's growth stage, the broader economic climate, and even its ownership model.

The common growth stages, as we mentioned in Chapter 5, are start-up, growth, maturity, and renewal/decline. In all of them, growth matters—growth *always* matters—but other drivers can be top of mind for leaders as the company moves through these stages.

- In the start-up stage, cash is typically the urgent focus, possibly superseding all other priorities.

- During the growth stage, a company will be laser-focused on growth but also on getting the right people in place and strengthening its profitability so that it can build assets and put itself in a position to take advantage of opportunities in the future.

- Mature companies that have sufficient cash, consistent profits, and asset strength have a solid foundation that allows them to concentrate on growth, people strategies, and harvesting more profits that can help move the company forward in the long term. They might work on improving the culture and finding other ways to attract the best talent.

- If the company begins to decline and leaders need to reinvent or renew it, they'll be focused on revenue growth and profit margin—specifically, how best to invest assets to improve profitability and how to reignite customer interest through innovation, breaking into new markets, or other strategic moves.

The ownership model of the company can influence the focus on drivers, too. A company that's privately owned may have a less intense focus on growth and profitability than a publicly owned company, where the leaders know their results will be scrutinized every quarter. A company that's owned by a venture capital firm will be under pressure to prioritize growth and profitability in order to produce a return on the investment the firm made when they bought the company. And yet, not all VC firms are the same. A number are now focused on supporting employee ownership models and sharing the profits with the people making the profits happen.

The final factors that can influence a company's performance and where the leaders are setting their sights are the external environment and the stock market.

The External Environment

While maximizing the 5 Drivers inside of the company is the central tenet of business acumen, leaders have to consider external factors when trying to make informed, effective decisions. The economy, competitors, industry issues, regulatory shifts, the political and social environment, a zombie apocalypse—all of which are outside of the company's control—can be critical to its success. Your fundamental grasp of the external environment helps you connect the dots for your own company and your customers and prospects.

External factors are the primary cause of cyclical changes in the growth or profitability of many organizations, because the overall economy tends to be cyclical and ever-changing. A company has to continually adjust, innovate, and even reinvent itself to keep pace with the shifting complexities. Most of these shifts are beyond the direct control or even influence of any company—even giants like Apple, BP, Microsoft, and Walmart.

For instance, in the United States, the Federal Reserve sets interest rates and influences the supply of money nationwide. Whether a small entrepreneur in her local community can get or afford a start-up loan or whether larger companies can raise capital to expand is heavily influenced by Federal Reserve policy. The availability and price of money affects the ability of all companies to invest in assets, innovate, take appropriate risks, and grow.

Of course, the COVID-19 pandemic is a perfect example of how companies can adapt (or not) to external factors that they can't control. While hotel and travel businesses struggled significantly, we saw some incredible growth in other areas: bikes, rollerblades, and other outdoor gear became hot commodities, often sold out for weeks and months on end. Companies that were able to shift their business models to support changed consumer interests and values thrived, while those that couldn't adapt floundered.

This just goes to show that the fact that business leaders can't control these external factors doesn't mean they're powerless. They can exercise their best business judgment by anticipating, preparing, and choosing the right strategic response. This is also an opportunity for *you* to add real value—by helping your clients through this strategic decision making. Ask yourself these questions:

- What changes are looming in the economy?
- What changes are about to take place in this company's industry?
- How will any of these changes potentially impact the 5 Business Drivers?
- How can I help them prepare for the threats and take advantage of the opportunities?

For instance, during an economic crisis, lots of companies focus more on cash so they can feel secure in their ability to ride out the worst of it, particularly when credit and capital are hard to come by. But what does it mean to focus on cash? Often it means conserving cash by cutting costs and investments to improve profitability, which could slow future growth. Understanding that your customers might be weighing this tradeoff is valuable insight.

The Stock Market   For public companies, the stock market is an external factor that plays an important role in directing the focus of the CEO and other leaders. They want the stock price to always be increasing, and when it's not, you'll see a lot of worried frowns. Why should they be concerned? First, because stock price is a reflection of the market's confidence in a company's future performance. People buy stock primarily because they believe they will make money as the price increases over time or through dividends. But a company also benefits in other ways when its stock price is higher:

- Acquisitions: When stock price is higher, the company can use fewer shares to buy another company.

- More cash: When a public company sells new shares to investors, it can sell a smaller percentage of the company to raise the same or greater amount of cash if the stock price is higher.

- Better credit ratings: One determinant of a public company's credit ratings relates to its stock price. With higher credit ratings, it can get loans at lower interest rates.

- Buy-out defense: A higher stock price is a defense against a takeover. As the stock price goes up, so does the company's value, and therefore its sales price.

Commit to an ongoing study of what's happening in the economy, in your industry and your customers' industries (more help with this in Part 2), and in the markets in which you operate. Your business acumen should include a working knowledge of how the external factors influencing the business world might influence both your own company and your customers.

SHIFTING WITH YOUR CUSTOMERS

Any time you impact any of the 5 Drivers, you are impacting the overall success of a company—your own, hopefully, and your client's. The question is, are you having the *maximum* impact and the *right* impact?

For instance, if the senior leaders in your company, some of your internal customers, say that profitability is all-important this quarter and ask employees to identify ways to reduce costs, you should certainly follow that lead. However, you have to apply your business acumen to make smart, productive decisions. Cutting costs too much could adversely affect product and service quality, reducing customer satisfaction and leading to lower sales and profits. And if you were responsible for increasing revenue to improve profitability, raising prices too high or using cash to launch product lines without sufficient research and analysis into customer tastes could result in lower sales and profits. As a salesperson, you might be tempted to go after customers who aren't a great fit for your products and services, creating trouble down the road.

All of this is equally true in your role with customers. Even if they're currently prioritizing one driver, you can help them keep the big picture in mind as you explore the nuanced benefits and applications of your products and services. And if you can do that, you can differentiate yourself and your products and services, proving your value to your clients and your own organization. In Part 2, we'll give you resources to make this kind of business acumen and big-picture perspective part of your next sales conversation.

› › › › › *THE BIG PICTURE IN REVIEW*

» The big picture is the overall perspective of how your company makes money through all 5 Drivers, within the context of the outside business and economic environment.

» All 5 Drivers are interdependent. Any impact on one affects the others. Companies known for excellence in one driver usually excel in others as well.

» At the same time, leaders shift their focus between the 5 Drivers over time based on a number of factors, including the development and maturity of the company, the ownership model, and the external environment.

» Business performance is affected by dynamic, complex forces in the external environment, including economic cycles, swings in the stock market, geopolitical shifts, regulatory changes, social shifts, etc.

» Anything you can do to impact any of the 5 Drivers influences the big picture. This is true for your own company and also your clients and customers. Key questions to ask are "Do I know what the priority is?" and "How can I impact that driver?"

PART 2

RESOURCES FOR SUCCESS IN YOUR NEXT SALES CONVERSATION

3 Steps for Aligning Your Value Proposition with Your Client's Business Objectives

"To learn and not to do is really not to learn. To know and not to do is really not to know." —Stephen R. Covey, The 7 Habits of Highly Effective People

JUST IN CASE WE HAVEN'T MADE IT crystal clear yet, your success as a salesperson—and your odds of hitting and exceeding your goals—relies on your ability to speak your customer's language, understand their strategy, and know how they're performing on their key metrics. We've given you a strong foundation in the business acumen you need, and in this part of the book, we're going to help you get granular and start analyzing your specific clients and prospects.

In all our work with sales teams, we've found that the sales process at many companies may vary depending on the nature of the customers and products. But across the board, one thing has been true: Those who consistently analyze their client's strategic focus through the drivers and understand the company's priorities build trust, add value, and engage in more productive conversations. And consequently, they close more and bigger sales and develop stronger partnerships with their clients. Because once you've analyzed a company's performance and communication, you're better prepared to identify their greatest challenges, develop a plan for helping them solve those challenges or successfully execute their strategies, and align your value proposition and conversations with their business needs.

And no matter where you are in the process with a customer, doing this work will have a positive impact on every next step. So go to SellingtheBigPicture.com and download the 3-Step Alignment tool and dive in.

STEP 1: ANALYZE YOUR CLIENT'S FOCUS AND FINANCIAL PERFORMANCE

Your Customer's Focus on the 5 Business Drivers

There are many resources for analyzing your client's business performance and strategic focus. These include:

- Your **discussions with your client.** Have they described their goals or financial focus? Are they focused on growth, decreasing costs, trying to drive cash flow, or improving operational efficiencies? And what actions are they taking? This is valuable information and something that is reasonable to ask your client in the course of your discussions.

- For clients that are publicly traded, the transcript of **the most recent earnings call** and especially the CEO's or CFO's prepared remarks. An earnings call is a conference call the CEO holds for investors and press outlining the company's quarterly results and explaining any big wins or challenges. As one of our instructors likes to say in our courses, these are moments when the CEO is shouting into the marketplace, "This is how to sell to us!"

- The **CEO's letter to shareholders**, or any internal strategy document you can get access to, is also helpful.

- With this information, use the following executive alignment activity to get a sense of which of the 5 Drivers your client is most focused on. If there is little to no information available for your client, do this exercise for a couple of other companies in the same industry to understand the themes and key metrics your client is likely focused on.

Your Customer's Financial Performance

To help you collect, analyze, and compare the most important measures—those we've covered in the chapters in Part 1—we've developed the Navigating the Financials worksheet we share in this resource. **You can access it in an easy-to-use format at SellingtheBigPicture.com.**

On this worksheet, you will notice that we have highlighted three numbers: revenue growth, net income (profit) growth, and the net profit margin. If you are short on time, start with these three measures. And ideally, you want to see revenues growing, profits growing faster, and profit margins higher than their peers. If your client's financials are not available, you may be able to get a sense of these from your client conversations. For nearly every company, these represent the three most important financial measures.

- Using a website that provides detailed financial information for your client's three financial statements, complete the worksheet. For the people driver, make note of any people challenges or successes that might be influencing the financial metrics, based on executive communication or news you read.

- If you go to SellingtheBigPicture.com, you can download a version of the Navigating the Financials Worksheet that includes a comparison column. You can use the comparison column for data from your client's prior period results to help you spot trends, or for a competitor's numbers or the client's industry averages to help you better understand their performance. You can use the S&P 500 industry averages in Resource 3. If your client does not share their financial information, use a publicly traded competitor or similar company to get a sense of what their financial picture might look like.

NAVIGATING THE FINANCIALS THROUGH THE 5 DRIVERS

	KEY METRIC	STATEMENT	EQUATION & YOUR NUMBERS	RESULTS
CASH	1) Cash & Cash Equivalents — Line Item: Cash & Cash Equivalents	Income / Balance / Cash Flow	No Equation	$
	2) Cash from Operations — Line Item: Cash from Operations	Income / Balance / Cash Flow	No Equation	$
PROFIT	3) Total Revenue — Line Item: Total Revenue	Income / Balance / Cash Flow	No Equation	$
	4) Net Income — Line Item: Net Income	Income / Balance / Cash Flow	No Equation	$
	5) Net Profit Margin — Line Item: Net Income / Total Revenue	Income / Balance / Cash Flow	Equation $\left(\dfrac{\text{Net Income}}{\text{Total Revenue}}\right) \times 100$ Your Numbers $\left(\dfrac{\quad}{\quad}\right) \times 100$	%
ASSETS	6) Equity Ratio — Line Item: Total Shareholder Equity / Total Assets	Income / Balance / Cash Flow	Equation $\left(\dfrac{\text{Total Shareholder Equity}}{\text{Total Assets}}\right) \times 100$ Your Numbers $\left(\dfrac{\quad}{\quad}\right) \times 100$	%
	7) Return on Assets (ROA) — Line Item: Net Income / Total Assets	Income / Balance / Cash Flow	Equation $\left(\dfrac{\text{Net Income}}{\text{Total Assets}}\right) \times 100$ Your Numbers $\left(\dfrac{\quad}{\quad}\right) \times 100$	%
GROWTH	8) Revenue Growth — Line Item: Total Revenue	Income / Balance / Cash Flow	Equation $\left(\dfrac{\text{*This Year's Total Revenue}}{\text{*Last Year's Total Revenue}} - 1\right) \times 100$ Your Numbers $\left(\dfrac{\quad}{\quad} - 1\right) \times 100$	%
	9) Net Income Growth — Line Item: Net Income	Income / Balance / Cash Flow	Equation $\left(\dfrac{\text{*This Year's Net Income}}{\text{*Last Year's Net Income}} - 1\right) \times 100$ Your Numbers $\left(\dfrac{\quad}{\quad} - 1\right) \times 100$	%
	10) Earnings Per Share (EPS) Growth — Line Item: Diluted EPS	Income / Balance / Cash Flow	Equation $\left(\dfrac{\text{*This Year's Diluted EPS}}{\text{*Last Year's Diluted EPS}} - 1\right) \times 100$ Your Numbers $\left(\dfrac{\quad}{\quad} - 1\right) \times 100$	%
PEOPLE	Key insights about people—internal and external stakeholders—that might influence other drivers and metrics:			

Note: Although we've included the essential metrics that can shed light on the 5 Drivers for just about any company, companies in some industries might rely on slightly different metrics. Consider adjusting the worksheet if you primarily serve clients in industries with unique measures of success. We describe some of these in Resource 3 where we offer an industry-level analysis of the 5 Drivers for 25 major sectors.

Answer these questions:

- Where is your client performing well? Where is the company struggling? How does their performance compare to the industry averages? (See Resource 3 for averages by industry.)

- How does that align with what you gathered from the executive communications analysis above?

As you're doing this work, take a moment to read our short Resource 2 on the priorities people in different functions or roles have when it comes to the 5 Drivers.

STEP 2: ALIGN YOUR SOLUTION TO YOUR CLIENT'S BUSINESS NEEDS

Based on your *communication with your client* and the information you gathered in Step 1, identify value propositions that capture how your product or service will help them address their key business objectives, challenges, and/or strategies, using the grid we've provided.

Build a Powerful, Aligned Value Proposition

Your Client's Business Objectives, Challenges, and Strategies	Your Solution

STEP 3: ACT

Based upon everything you've learned, what are the next three actions you need to take with this customer to move the partnership forward? Again, building your functional awareness of your contact's needs and focus can help you be more effective (see Resource 2).

Who	What	When

Function: What Does the Person You're Talking to Care About?

"The royal road to a person's heart is to talk about the things he or she treasures most."[15] —Dale Carnegie

DO YOU REMEMBER THE STORY IN CHAPTER 5 about the salesperson who sold patient-monitoring devices to hospitals? When she pitched to nursing staff and physicians, she focused on the benefits to patients and overworked nurses. But when she understood the effects of readmission rates on the hospital's profit, she elevated her conversation to the chief nursing officer, who was in charge of controlling costs, improving patient care, and reducing readmissions. She planned different conversations for different roles based on what the people in those roles cared about most.

As a salesperson, you're always under time pressure. You know the person you're talking to feels like they need to get on with the next important thing on their to-do list, so you simplify your sales approach to the most essential and efficient conversation. This can be especially true when you're trying to get multiple people or departments in a client organization on the same page when it comes to your product or service.

With these pressures to be efficient and clear, it can be easy to overlook the fact that different people in different roles in different divisions, departments, and teams have different cares or concerns, and focus on the 5 Business Drivers in different ways. That's how they contribute to the success of the organization as a whole and work together to fulfill a unifying purpose and vision.

As the person selling to them, you need to be prepared to understand both the big-picture growth strategy *and* the differences in perspectives. The further down you go in an organization, the more difficult this can be because the gap between the enterprise-wide goals and the tactical challenges of the person you're trying to partner with gets wider. So how do you leverage your business acumen to create value for people at different levels? You can connect the dots for them—between your solution, their specific problems, and overall business results. When you do, you'll help your contact shine within their organization, building their own credibility and delivering better results in their role. And you'll prepare them to sell your solution internally to key decision makers—dramatically increasing your chances of closing the deal.

But first, you have to meet your customer where they are. If you're having the exact same conversation with every person, regardless of their role or function, you're missing an opportunity to connect and align with their needs. Talking about employee satisfaction might excite a human resources officer, but the same pitch will get you an impatient yawn from a finance manager. However, discussing return on investment, efficient use of assets, and expense reductions will make the finance manager perk up. To help you prepare for your next conversation, we've provided a simple table summarizing which of the 5 Drivers people in different roles tend to care about most.

For each of your customers, partners, and contacts, earn the right to share your solutions and ideas by taking the time to consider or uncover what matters to them most. Develop answers to the following, based on what you know about your clients and contacts:

- Which business driver do they focus on?
- What are their current strategies to boost performance on that driver?

- How does their performance impact company goals and objectives?

The information we shared in this chapter is just a helpful starting point. Dig for your customer's unique challenges and goals. Cater to them. Customize your presentations and conversations for them. And you will be on the royal road to that person's heart, to paraphrase Dale Carnegie.

Role/Function and Driver Focus

Role or Function	Drivers in Focus
CEO and senior executives	· All 5 Drivers—they're all the responsibility of high-level leaders · Growth and profit will usually be top priorities, especially in publicly traded companies · The driver most in focus at the moment can shift based on circumstances · They're the group most concerned about shareholders
Mid-level leaders and managers	· People—well-functioning teams that deliver on the other drivers · Profit—controlling costs and/or growing revenue depending on the specific department · Growth
Operations	· Assets—especially the utilization of assets · People—focused on developing processes and systems that help people do efficient, quality work · Profit—controlling costs through efficiencies across departments and divisions
Finance and accounting	· Cash—cash flow · Profit—profit margin · Assets—asset strength and utilization
Purchasing	· Profit—controlling costs! · Assets—return on investment
Customer service and support	· People—customers, of course · Profit—controlling costs
Sales and marketing	· People—customers · Growth—especially in revenue and profit
Human resources	· People—employees · Profit—efficient, well-trained teams that keep costs under control · Growth—onboarding employees faster and with the right skills, to support the company's growth objectives

Your Customer's Context: The 5 Business Drivers by Industry

AS WE'VE ALREADY SAID, YOUR CUSTOMER DOESN'T operate in a vacuum. The broader business environment influences how they operate, what kinds of results they might expect, and what kinds of challenges they might be trying to solve.

In the following pages, we're going to give you important contextual clues about that environment. For each of the major 25 industries, we'll share a one-page guide to nuances of the 5 Drivers and industry averages for important metrics, drawn from the 500 companies in the S&P 500. Whether it's the thin margins retailers live with, the serious employee challenges healthcare providers struggle to solve, or some of the industry-specific metrics you might want to look at, we'll give you more context for assessing your customers' results.

Note: Because cash measures can vary dramatically from company to company based on a company's overall "size," industry averages don't mean much. We've presented the numbers as a percentage of sales. Like other similar metrics—for instance, profit margin—we've divided the cash metric by total revenue or sales and then multiplied by 100.

You can come back to this part of the book over and over as you work with new clients in new industries, giving you a higher level of business acumen. Apply it and you'll see higher-level results.

AEROSPACE AND DEFENSE

Highlights

- Aerospace and defense contractors typically work with a small number of unique, powerful customers—often government agencies—who dominate the market. These customers are sometimes called monopsonies or monopoly buyers because they are the only or primary buyers in the industry. This dynamic creates a very different kind of contractor-customer relationship, in which the **customers**
  - Control terms and pricing
  - Drive competition between contractors through bidding processes
  - Won't work exclusively with one contractor on a program
  - Sometimes set the allowed profit margin or the overall size of the deal or program
- While the companies in this industry are some of the most innovative in the world, they **do not have margins as high** as other innovative businesses, such as medical and technology innovators, primarily because defense contractor innovations are often co-created with or co-funded by their customers.
- This industry **attracts top talent** with highly specific skill sets and backgrounds, and it's especially competitive against other tech innovators in tight labor markets.
- Instead of the traditional operating margin metric, many companies in this space use a similar metric called return on sales (ROS).

For current industry data, go to SellingtheBigPicture.com.

Compare your client's results to industry and S&P 500 results.

	Aerospace and Defense Industry Avg.	S&P 500 Avg.
CASH		
Cash and Cash Equivalents as a % of Sales	20.9%	22.7%
Cash Generated from Operations as a % of Sales	10.3%	20.9%
PROFIT		
Gross Profit Margin %	25.5%	49.6%
Operating Profit Margin %	9.5%	23.2%
Net Profit Margin %	5.2%	12.9%
ASSETS		
Return on Assets (ROA) %	4.1%	8.4%
Equity Ratio	29.2%	33.7%
GROWTH		
Revenue Growth Rate %	5.8%	6.3%
Net Income Growth Rate %	14.1%	8.1%
PEOPLE		
Revenue per Employee	$1.8M	$1.6M

Notes:
- Because cash amounts can vary dramatically from company to company based on a company's overall "size," we've presented the numbers as a percentage of sales or revenue: the cash metric divided by total revenue or sales and then multiplied by 100.
- S&P 500 averages are calculated based on 3 years of annual reports as of July 2024, rounded. However, because certain financial industries, like asset management companies and diversified banks, hold large amounts of cash, they have been removed from the cash calculations.
- Most industry or sector averages are also calculated based on 3 years of annual reports from S&P 500 companies. However, certain companies or subsectors in the S&P sometimes skew the data far from what is typical for an industry, so we have occasionally removed some companies or subsectors or changed periods in our calculations to provide a more accurate set of comparison data.

AUTOMOBILE MANUFACTURING

Highlights

- Due to challenges with electric vehicles (prices, battery life and safety, charging times, etc.), hybrids and internal combustion engine (ICE) vehicles are seeing a comeback. Companies that stockpiled parts for EVs could have some **asset challenges**, leading to more competitive pricing and **reduced profit margins**.

- **Profit margins** tend to be low (often less than 10 percent) in the auto manufacturing business, but unique or ultra-luxury brands can achieve significantly higher margins—like Ferrari's 23 percent in 2024. In the data shown here, notice average net profit margin is greater than average operating profit margin, which could be a result of profits from investments in other businesses, finance income from manufacturers, foreign exchange gains from overseas sales and operations, or interest income. All are below the operating income line, potentially causing net income to be greater.

- Companies in the automotive industry keep quite a bit of **cash and cash equivalents** on hand. **Cash flow**, however, is typically lower.

- Subscription models are becoming more popular in the auto industry, helping with **customer retention** and brand satisfaction.

For current industry data, go to SellingtheBigPicture.com.

Compare your client's results to industry and S&P 500 results.

	Automobile Industry Avg.	S&P 500 Avg.
CASH		
Cash and Cash Equivalents as a % of Sales	15.2%	22.7%
Cash Generated from Operations as a % of Sales	10.7%	20.9%
PROFIT		
Gross Profit Margin %	18.0%	49.6%
Operating Profit Margin %	7.0%	23.2%
Net Profit Margin %	7.3%	12.9%
ASSETS		
Return on Assets (ROA) %	5.0%	8.4%
Equity Ratio	34.4%	33.7%
GROWTH		
Revenue Growth Rate %	8.1%	6.3%
Net Income Growth Rate %	9.0%	8.1%
PEOPLE		
Revenue per Employee	$5.8M	$1.6M

Notes:

- Because cash amounts can vary dramatically from company to company based on a company's overall "size," we've presented the numbers as a percentage of sales or revenue: the cash metric divided by total revenue or sales and then multiplied by 100.
- S&P 500 averages are calculated based on 3 years of annual reports as of July 2024, rounded. However, because certain financial industries, like asset management companies and diversified banks, hold large amounts of cash, they have been removed from the cash calculations.
- Most industry or sector averages are also calculated based on 3 years of annual reports from S&P 500 companies. However, certain companies or subsectors in the S&P sometimes skew the data far from what is typical for an industry, so we have occasionally removed some companies or subsectors or changed periods in our calculations to provide a more accurate set of comparison data.

COMPUTER HARDWARE

Highlights

- Computer hardware companies often experience **moderate to high profit margins**, depending on their level of innovation and pricing power.

- Established players generate **significant cash flow**, driven by high-margin products and strong operational efficiencies. New entrants might have weaker cash flow due to high capital expenditure.

- For hardware tied to ecosystems (such as Apple or Microsoft products that work together seamlessly), customer retention rates are crucial to measuring brand loyalty and the ecosystem's stickiness.

- Companies in this industry often maintain **substantial fixed assets**, including advanced manufacturing facilities and proprietary production equipment. Intellectual property (patents, designs, and trademarks) is also a vital asset, protecting innovation and ensuring competitive advantage.

- Effective inventory management is critical due to the risk of obsolescence, as rapid technological advancement can quickly render products outdated.

- R&D as a percentage of revenue is tracked carefully and typically falls between 8% and 15%.

For current industry data, go to SellingtheBigPicture.com.

Compare your client's results to industry and S&P 500 results.

	Computer Hardware Industry Avg.	S&P 500 Avg.
CASH		
Cash and Cash Equivalents as a % of Sales	23.7%	22.7%
Cash Generated from Operations as a % of Sales	27.5%	20.9%
PROFIT		
Gross Profit Margin %	56.1%	49.6%
Operating Profit Margin %	22%	23.2%
Net Profit Margin %	17.8%	12.9%
ASSETS		
Return on Assets (ROA) %	12.4%	8.4%
Equity Ratio	38.7%	33.7%
GROWTH		
Revenue Growth Rate %	5.9%	6.3%
Net Income Growth Rate %	8.2%	8.1%
PEOPLE		
Revenue per Employee	$1.2M	$1.6M

Notes:

- Because cash amounts can vary dramatically from company to company based on a company's overall "size," we've presented the numbers as a percentage of sales or revenue: the cash metric divided by total revenue or sales and then multiplied by 100.

- S&P 500 averages are calculated based on 3 years of annual reports as of July 2024, rounded. However, because certain financial industries, like asset management companies and diversified banks, hold large amounts of cash, they have been removed from the cash calculations.

- Most industry or sector averages are also calculated based on 3 years of annual reports from S&P 500 companies. However, certain companies or subsectors in the S&P sometimes skew the data far from what is typical for an industry, so we have occasionally removed some companies or subsectors or changed periods in our calculations to provide a more accurate set of comparison data.

CONSUMER DISCRETIONARY SECTOR

Highlights

- Discretionary, nonessential goods—including luxury goods, travel and leisure, and home improvement—are purchased based on consumer preferences, lifestyle, and income.

- The sector can be heavily affected by economic trends because demand reflects **consumer confidence and spending habits**. Investors even use the sector as a barometer for the overall health of the economy.

- Success relies on strong branding, quality products, and alignment with consumer trends. **Gross margins** will be impacted by how much an organization prioritizes quality, uniqueness, and innovation.

- One **key asset metric** that consumer discretionary companies measure is inventory days on hand (DOH), which measures how quickly a company sells its inventory. A slower turnover might indicate issues like poor product selection, lack of innovation, or misalignment with customer needs.

For current industry data, go to SellingtheBigPicture.com.

Compare your client's results to industry and S&P 500 results.

	Consumer Discretionary Sector Avg.	S&P 500 Avg.
CASH		
Cash and Cash Equivalents as a % of Sales	37.3%	22.7%
Cash Generated from Operations as a % of Sales	-0.6%	20.9%
PROFIT		
Gross Profit Margin %	34.8%	49.6%
Operating Profit Margin %	2.3%	23.2%
Net Profit Margin %	-18.4%	12.9%
ASSETS		
Return on Assets (ROA) %	10.3%	8.4%
Equity Ratio	17.5%	33.7%
GROWTH		
Revenue Growth Rate %	13.8%	6.3%
Net Income Growth Rate %	17.6%	8.1%
PEOPLE		
Revenue per Employee	$1.7M	$1.6M

Notes:

- Because cash amounts can vary dramatically from company to company based on a company's overall "size," we've presented the numbers as a percentage of sales or revenue: the cash metric divided by total revenue or sales and then multiplied by 100.

- S&P 500 averages are calculated based on 3 years of annual reports as of July 2024, rounded. However, because certain financial industries, like asset management companies and diversified banks, hold large amounts of cash, they have been removed from the cash calculations.

- Most industry or sector averages are also calculated based on 3 years of annual reports from S&P 500 companies. However, certain companies or subsectors in the S&P sometimes skew the data far from what is typical for an industry, so we have occasionally removed some companies or subsectors or changed periods in our calculations to provide a more accurate set of comparison data.

CONSUMER ELECTRONICS

Highlights

- Innovation is key for consumer electronics companies. They invest a substantial amount of their revenue into R&D to help them develop groundbreaking products. Two key areas of focus are connectivity and integration of emerging technologies such as artificial intelligence (AI), internet of things (IoT), and augmented reality (AR).

- Successful and mature consumer electronics organizations have **high profit margins** and generate **significant cash flow**.

- Early lifecycle consumer electronics organizations have lower margins but **substantial growth potential**.

- An additional metric that companies in this industry track is balance of share (BOS), which indicates what percentage of the product market they own (TVs, smartphones, etc.).

For current industry data, go to SellingtheBigPicture.com.

Compare your client's results to industry and S&P 500 results.

	Consumer Electronics industry Avg.	S&P 500 Avg.
CASH		
Cash and Cash Equivalents as a % of Sales	9.6%	22.7%
Cash Generated from Operations as a % of Sales	28.4%	20.9%
PROFIT		
Gross Profit Margin %	41.8%	49.6%
Operating Profit Margin %	29.8%	23.2%
Net Profit Margin %	25.9%	12.9%
ASSETS		
Return on Assets (ROA) %	28.1%	8.4%
Equity Ratio	17%	33.7%
GROWTH		
Revenue Growth Rate %	1.6%	6.3%
Net Income Growth Rate %	0.8%	8.1%
PEOPLE		
Revenue per Employee	$20.2M	$1.6M

Notes:

- Because cash amounts can vary dramatically from company to company based on a company's overall "size," we've presented the numbers as a percentage of sales or revenue: the cash metric divided by total revenue or sales and then multiplied by 100.
- S&P 500 averages are calculated based on 3 years of annual reports as of July 2024, rounded. However, because certain financial industries, like asset management companies and diversified banks, hold large amounts of cash, they have been removed from the cash calculations.
- Most industry or sector averages are also calculated based on 3 years of annual reports from S&P 500 companies. However, certain companies or subsectors in the S&P sometimes skew the data far from what is typical for an industry, so we have occasionally removed some companies or subsectors or changed periods in our calculations to provide a more accurate set of comparison data.

FINANCIAL SERVICES, BANKS

Highlights

- Banks make money in two basic ways:
  - Lending money at a higher rate than the interest they pay on customers' deposits.
  - Charging fees for other services they provide to banking customers, commercial and consumer—payment and money transfers, specialty accounts, wealth management, and more. These services are attractive because they're often high value, low cost, and less volatile than lending.
- Cost management is extremely important for banks because they can carry high costs for IT and cybersecurity, human resources, and operating physical branches.
- Due to the nature of banking, common metrics for other industries don't always apply or aren't the best basis for assessing performance. Instead, banks track the following:
  - **Cash**—Common equity tier 1 (CET1) capital ratio: a bank's core capital as a percentage of risk-weighted assets. It's a measure of financial strength, so it could be an asset measure, but banks carry so much cash that they don't track it all on its own. The CET1 capital ratio reflects a bank's ability to absorb shocks, such as loan defaults, the same way cash measures do. It's required by regulatory agencies. Higher is better—to a point—because it indicates that the bank has more secure, stable, quality capital.
  - **Profit**—Net interest income: the amount of income earned from interest charged on loans minus the interest paid on deposits to customers. Net interest margin is net interest income as a percentage of the bank's interest-earning assets.
  - **Profit**—Expense or efficiency ratio: administrative costs as a percentage of the bank's total revenue (net interest income plus non-interest income). Lower is better.

- **Assets**—Non-performing loans ratio: the ratio of non-performing loans to total loans. Lower is better.
- **Assets**—Loan-to-deposit ratio: this ratio varies depending on size and strategy. Larger banks tend to have lower ratios because they have a high volume of deposits.

For current industry data, go to SellingtheBigPicture.com.

Compare your client's results to industry and S&P 500 results.

	Banking industry Avg.	S&P 500 Avg.
CASH		
CET1 Capital Ratio %	Larger banks: 11% Smaller banks: 14%	NA
PROFIT		
Net Interest Margin %	3.0%	NA
Efficiency Ratio %	Larger banks: 52% Smaller banks: up to 70%	NA
ASSETS		
Non-Performing Loans Ratio %	1%	NA
Loan-to-Deposit Ratio %	65% to 90%, depending on size and strategy	NA
Return on Assets (ROA) %	1.3%	8.4%
Equity Ratio	11.1%	33.7%
GROWTH		
Revenue Growth Rate %	6.0%	6.3%
Net Income Growth Rate %	5.0%	8.1%
PEOPLE		
Revenue per Employee	$610,800	$1.6M

Notes:
- S&P 500 averages are calculated based on 3 years of annual reports as of July 2024, rounded. However, because certain financial industries, like asset management companies and diversified banks, hold large amounts of cash, they have been removed from the cash calculations.
- Industry averages are primarily based on research and data from other sources, although some are based on S&P 500 companies in the regional banks industry.

HEALTH INSURERS

Highlights

- Health insurers have **thin profit margins** because of high pay-outs to providers, significant operating costs to support their members (insured customers), and heavy competition that limits their ability to raise prices.

- The more **members** a company has, the more **cash flow** they generate, and the more they can invest in technology and marketing to **grow their revenues**.

- Healthcare insurers are focused on maximizing operating efficiencies, building relationships with their **networks of providers**, and pricing their insurance plans appropriately to reflect the risk and utilization they estimate within their membership base.

- They often **carry less pure cash** on their balance sheets than the S&P average, but they do carry a lot of **highly liquid assets**, like marketable securities and other short-term investments, they could turn to cash quickly as a reserve against the claims they will have to pay in the future. Government regulations require them to ensure they can cover members' medical costs in extreme cases.

- An additional key measure is the medical loss ratio, or benefit expense ratio, typically between 80 and 85 percent. This is the percentage of member premium payments that are then used to pay for healthcare benefits for the member.

For current industry data, go to SellingtheBigPicture.com.

Compare your client's results to industry and S&P 500 results.

	Health Insurance Industry Avg.	S&P 500 Avg.
CASH		
Cash and Cash Equivalents as a % of Sales	6.8%	22.7%
Cash Generated from Operations as a % of Sales	5.4%	20.9%
PROFIT		
Gross Profit Margin %	29.4%	49.6%
Operating Profit Margin %	5.3%	23.2%
Net Profit Margin %	3.3%	12.9%
ASSETS		
Return on Assets (ROA) %	5.3%	8.4%
Equity Ratio	32.5%	33.7%
GROWTH		
Revenue Growth Rate %	7.1%	6.3%
Net Income Growth Rate %	6.9%	8.1%
PEOPLE		
Revenue per Employee	$8.9M	$1.6M

Notes:

- Because cash amounts can vary dramatically from company to company based on a company's overall "size," we've presented the numbers as a percentage of sales or revenue: the cash metric divided by total revenue or sales and then multiplied by 100.
- S&P 500 averages are calculated based on 3 years of annual reports as of July 2024, rounded. However, because certain financial industries, like asset management companies and diversified banks, hold large amounts of cash, they have been removed from the cash calculations.
- Most industry or sector averages are also calculated based on 3 years of annual reports from S&P 500 companies. However, certain companies or subsectors in the S&P sometimes skew the data far from what is typical for an industry, so we have occasionally removed some companies or subsectors or changed periods in our calculations to provide a more accurate set of comparison data.

HEALTHCARE, PROVIDERS AND HOSPITALS

Highlights

- **Profit margins are very thin** in this industry due to extensive **people** and supply costs, along with significant investments in **assets** such as equipment, facilities, and technology. Medical practices often have a net profit margin below 5%.

- Providers make an effort to minimize costs by **using assets** as effectively and efficiently as possible to generate better return on assets, which in turn generates enough **cash flow** to grow and expand operations.

- Healthcare providers care deeply about **patient outcomes** and are partially compensated by insurers, governments, and patients based on the quality of care.

- Companies in this industry **carry very little cash**, as much of it is being put to use in their infrastructure, in employing the best **physicians and care teams**, and into **growth** into new therapeutic or geographic areas.

- A key measure healthcare providers track to keep a lid on operating costs is **free cash flow**—how much cash they generate from operations after factoring in investments into assets. And because of the lag between when they provide care and when they're paid by insurers and sometimes patients (often months), they pay close attention to revenue cycle management.

For current industry data, go to SellingtheBigPicture.com.

Compare your client's results to industry and S&P 500 results.

	Healthcare Provider Industry Avg.	S&P 500 Avg.
CASH		
Cash and Cash Equivalents as a % of Sales	2.7%	22.7%
Cash Generated from Operations as a % of Sales	13%	20.9%
PROFIT		
Gross Profit Margin %	35%	49.6%
Operating Profit Margin %	5%	23.2%
Net Profit Margin %	2%	12.9%
ASSETS		
Return on Assets (ROA) %	9.1%	8.4%
Equity Ratio	18.6%	33.7%
GROWTH		
Revenue Growth Rate %	3%	6.3%
Net Income Growth Rate %	-10%	8.1%
PEOPLE		
Revenue per Employee	$1.5M	$1.6M

Notes:

- Because cash amounts can vary dramatically from company to company based on a company's overall "size," we've presented the numbers as a percentage of sales or revenue: the cash metric divided by total revenue or sales and then multiplied by 100.
- S&P 500 averages are calculated based on 3 years of annual reports as of July 2024, rounded. However, because certain financial industries, like asset management companies and diversified banks, hold large amounts of cash, they have been removed from the cash calculations.
- Most industry or sector averages are also calculated based on 3 years of annual reports from S&P 500 companies. However, certain companies or subsectors in the S&P sometimes skew the data far from what is typical for an industry, so we have occasionally removed some companies or subsectors or changed periods in our calculations to provide a more accurate set of comparison data.

HOSPITALITY

Highlights

- Hospitality includes a large array of businesses that offer services including lodging, food and beverage, and travel and tourism.

- **Profitability** in this industry is greatly affected by overall economic factors, as businesses and consumers tend to reduce hospitality consumption in times of economic downturn.

- **Profit margins are shrinking** on average within the industry due to increased labor costs as companies realize they must **raise pay to attract and keep top talent**. Consequently, they're highly focused on both efficiency and providing quality service to continue to attract customers.

- Key measures for companies that provide lodging include average daily rate (ADR) and revenue per available room (RevPAR).

For current industry data, go to SellingtheBigPicture.com.

Compare your client's results to industry and S&P 500 results.

	Hospitality Industry Avg.	S&P 500 Avg.
CASH		
Cash and Cash Equivalents as a % of Sales	18.1%	22.7%
Cash Generated from Operations as a % of Sales	5.2%	20.9%
PROFIT		
Gross Profit Margin %	54.2%	49.6%
Operating Profit Margin %	17.5%	23.2%
Net Profit Margin %	7.5%	12.9%
ASSETS		
Return on Assets (ROA) %	3.5%	8.4%
Equity Ratio	0.1%	33.7%
GROWTH		
Revenue Growth Rate %	20.3%	6.3%
Net Income Growth Rate %	40.9%	8.1%
PEOPLE		
Revenue per Employee	$0.5M	$1.6M

Notes:

- Because cash amounts can vary dramatically from company to company based on a company's overall "size," we've presented the numbers as a percentage of sales or revenue: the cash metric divided by total revenue or sales and then multiplied by 100.
- S&P 500 averages are calculated based on 3 years of annual reports as of July 2024, rounded. However, because certain financial industries, like asset management companies and diversified banks, hold large amounts of cash, they have been removed from the cash calculations.
- Most industry or sector averages are also calculated based on 3 years of annual reports from S&P 500 companies. However, certain companies or subsectors in the S&P sometimes skew the data far from what is typical for an industry, so we have occasionally removed some companies or subsectors or changed periods in our calculations to provide a more accurate set of comparison data.

INSURANCE, PROPERTY AND CASUALTY AND LIFE

Highlights

- Insurance companies depend on complex actuarial models to calculate their expected losses (claims) and the timing of those losses. They regularly update these estimates to account for changing risks and economic conditions and to ensure they can meet future claims, which they can do primarily because they collect premiums in the present and investing the cash. Often, the money made off the investments is a sizeable portion of their earnings.

- They're required by regulation to have a **high level of liquid assets**, although not necessarily cash, compared to other industries to pay current and future claims.

- The number of policies in force is a key driver of performance and **growth**.

- Insurance companies measure **profitability** through three key ratios: The *loss ratio* is the total claims and loss adjustment expenses paid over a specific period divided by the premiums collected over that period, and shows whether the company is earning a profit from underwriting, The *expense ratio* is the expense of acquiring, underwriting, and servicing policies divided by the premiums collected on those policies, and measures operational efficiency. The *combined ratio* (the combination of the two) indicates overall profitability. Combined ratios nearing and over 100 put pressure on a company's earnings.

- Decisions in property and casualty (P&C) companies have a much shorter term outlook, assessing premiums compared to expected claims in the next year. Life insurance companies operate on a much longer timeframe, because they're making long-term investment decisions based on the life spans and mortality rates of their customer base.

For current industry data, go to SellingtheBigPicture.com.

Compare your client's results to industry and S&P 500 results.

	Insurance Industry Avg.	S&P 500 Avg.
CASH		
Cash and Cash Equivalents as a % of Sales	P&C: 8.6%; Life: 19.6%	22.7%
Cash Generated from Operations as a % of Sales	21.4%	20.9%
PROFIT		
Gross Profit Margin %	31.5%	49.6%
Operating Profit Margin %	16.2%	23.2%
Net Profit Margin %	11.9%	12.9%
ASSETS		
Return on Assets (ROA) %	P&C: 4.1%; Life: 1.6%	8.4%
Equity Ratio	P&C: 28.2%; Life: 16.4%	33.7%
GROWTH		
Revenue Growth Rate %	P&C: 8.8%; Life: 3.0%	6.3%
Net Income Growth Rate %	P&C: 4.9%; Life: 12.9%	8.1%
PEOPLE		
Revenue per Employee	$1.9M	$1.6M

Notes:

- Because cash amounts can vary dramatically from company to company based on a company's overall "size," we've presented the numbers as a percentage of sales or revenue: the cash metric divided by total revenue or sales and then multiplied by 100.
- S&P 500 averages are calculated based on 3 years of annual reports as of July 2024, rounded. However, because certain financial industries, like asset management companies and diversified banks, hold large amounts of cash, they have been removed from the cash calculations.
- Most industry or sector averages are also calculated based on 3 years of annual reports from S&P 500 companies. However, certain companies or subsectors in the S&P sometimes skew the data far from what is typical for an industry, so we have occasionally removed some companies or subsectors or changed periods in our calculations to provide a more accurate set of comparison data.

INFORMATION TECHNOLOGY SERVICES

Highlights

- The IT service industry includes companies that offer a range of products and services to other companies, primarily.

- **Employee teams** require high degrees of specialized knowledge, experience, and certifications to deliver customer solutions, which requires IT service companies to have a strong focus on attracting and retaining top talent. It's a dynamic, fast-changing industry, so employee development is critical to keep up with shifts in the market, technology, related industries, and client needs.

- Some companies develop proprietary systems that require investing in R&D.

- **Cash** is important to IT services companies for talent costs, developing new capabilities and service offerings, and marketing. **Cash flow** can be especially important because many companies hire contractors to meet shifting project needs.

- Although IT companies may generate high revenues through their services, the high cost of labor leads to **generally low profit margins**, and so they focus on building and managing efficient teams. They closely track **labor utilization** rates (keeping their employees highly billable). For many IT companies, small improvements in utilization rates can mean millions of dollars in incremental earnings.

For current industry data, go to SellingtheBigPicture.com.

Compare your client's results to industry and S&P 500 results.

	IT Services Industry Avg.	S&P 500 Avg.
CASH		
Cash and Cash Equivalents as a % of Sales	17.3%	22.7%
Cash Generated from Operations as a % of Sales	19.5%	20.9%
PROFIT		
Gross Profit Margin %	41.6%	49.6%
Operating Profit Margin %	17.5%	23.2%
Net Profit Margin %	11.4%	12.9%
ASSETS		
Return on Assets (ROA) %	7.2%	8.4%
Equity Ratio	33.2%	33.7%
GROWTH		
Revenue Growth Rate %	3.9%	6.3%
Net Income Growth Rate %	10.7%	8.1%
PEOPLE		
Revenue per Employee	$1.1M	$1.6M

Notes:

- Because cash amounts can vary dramatically from company to company based on a company's overall "size," we've presented the numbers as a percentage of sales or revenue: the cash metric divided by total revenue or sales and then multiplied by 100.
- S&P 500 averages are calculated based on 3 years of annual reports as of July 2024, rounded. However, because certain financial industries, like asset management companies and diversified banks, hold large amounts of cash, they have been removed from the cash calculations.
- Most industry or sector averages are also calculated based on 3 years of annual reports from S&P 500 companies. However, certain companies or subsectors in the S&P sometimes skew the data far from what is typical for an industry, so we have occasionally removed some companies, subsectors, or periods from our calculations to provide a more accurate set of comparison data.

MANUFACTURING

Highlights

- Manufacturing includes companies involved in the mechanical, physical, or chemical transformation of materials, substances, or components into new products. The manufacturing sector includes a vast array of subsectors including the manufacturing of food and beverage, textiles, apparel, chemical, plastics, metal, electronics, furniture, and more.

- Manufacturing companies face many challenges due to the rapid advancement of technology and the changing demands of sustainability, **customer** relations, and reshoring. The sector has also been shifting its source of **revenue** from business-to-business (B2B) sales toward direct-to-consumer (B2C) sales as technology allows manufacturers to more easily engage directly with customers.

- Companies in this industry make major investments of **cash and liquid assets**, called capital expenditures, into more fixed, **long-term assets** to keep manufacturing facilities up-to-date, efficient, and productive. They weigh market demand and ideal facility locations (to control transportation costs) to maximize **asset utilization**.

- They focus on minimizing downtime and reducing expenses from any inefficient, outdated processes to maximize their return on investment—and stay viable in a competitive industry.

- Some key measures for manufacturing include throughput, cycle time, contribution margin, and demand forecasting.

For current industry data, go to SellingtheBigPicture.com.

Compare your client's results to industry and S&P 500 results.

	Manufacturing Industry Avg.	S&P 500 Avg.
CASH		
Cash and Cash Equivalents as a % of Sales	14.5%	22.7%
Cash Generated from Operations as a % of Sales	16.5%	20.9%
PROFIT		
Gross Profit Margin %	39.5%	49.6%
Operating Profit Margin %	18.1%	23.2%
Net Profit Margin %	13.5%	12.9%
ASSETS		
Return on Assets (ROA) %	9.2%	8.4%
Equity Ratio	40.3%	33.7%
GROWTH		
Revenue Growth Rate %	5.2%	6.3%
Net Income Growth Rate %	7.7%	8.1%
PEOPLE		
Revenue per Employee	$0.6M	$1.6M

Notes:

- Because cash amounts can vary dramatically from company to company based on a company's overall "size," we've presented the numbers as a percentage of sales or revenue: the cash metric divided by total revenue or sales and then multiplied by 100.
- S&P 500 averages are calculated based on 3 years of annual reports as of July 2024, rounded. However, because certain financial industries, like asset management companies and diversified banks, hold large amounts of cash, they have been removed from the cash calculations.
- Most industry or sector averages are also calculated based on 3 years of annual reports from S&P 500 companies. However, certain companies or subsectors in the S&P sometimes skew the data far from what is typical for an industry, so we have occasionally removed some companies, subsectors, or periods from our calculations to provide a more accurate set of comparison data.

MINING

Highlights

- The mining industry operates on **lower profit margins** due to high capital expenditures in equipment, facilities, and production while relying heavily on global commodity prices that companies cannot control.

- Companies gather ore with heavy equipment and then process it, usually focusing on extracting one primary metal. **Revenue** is generated by selling the refined ore, for example, copper, gold, or iron. But the ore includes small amounts of other metals, such as silver, cobalt, etc., called byproducts. Mining companies often offset expenses by selling the most valuable byproducts.

- Mining is an **asset-intensive industry** focused on maximizing the efficiency of equipment and infrastructure to enhance returns on investment.

- **Cash flow** is cyclical, with high commodity prices enabling reinvestment in maintenance, new capital projects, and building financial resilience for periods of low pricing.

- Other key metrics include average realized price, unit cash cost, and **employee safety metrics** like total recordable incident rate.

For current industry data, go to SellingtheBigPicture.com.

Compare your client's results to industry and S&P 500 results.

	Mining Industry Avg.	S&P 500 Avg.
CASH		
Cash and Cash Equivalents as a % of Sales	11.1%	22.7%
Cash Generated from Operations as a % of Sales	18.2%	20.9%
PROFIT		
Gross Profit Margin %	31.3%	49.6%
Operating Profit Margin %	18.8%	23.2%
Net Profit Margin %	12.4%	12.9%
ASSETS		
Return on Assets (ROA) %	8.8%	8.4%
Equity Ratio	41.7%	33.7%
GROWTH		
Revenue Growth Rate %	2.8%	6.3%
Net Income Growth Rate %	4.2%	8.1%
PEOPLE		
Revenue per Employee	$0.9M	$1.6M

Notes:

- Because cash amounts can vary dramatically from company to company based on a company's overall "size," we've presented the numbers as a percentage of sales or revenue: the cash metric divided by total revenue or sales and then multiplied by 100.
- S&P 500 averages are calculated based on 3 years of annual reports as of July 2024, rounded. However, because certain financial industries, like asset management companies and diversified banks, hold large amounts of cash, they have been removed from the cash calculations.
- Most industry or sector averages are also calculated based on 3 years of annual reports from S&P 500 companies. However, certain companies or subsectors in the S&P sometimes skew the data far from what is typical for an industry, so we have occasionally removed some companies, subsectors, or periods from our calculations to provide a more accurate set of comparison data.

OIL AND GAS, UPSTREAM

Highlights

- The upstream oil and gas sector focuses on exploration and production (E&P), generating revenue by extracting crude oil and natural gas, with prices driven by global supply and demand.

- **Profits** in this industry depend on the gap between the average realized price per barrel of oil equivalent (BOE) and the cost of exploration and production. The upstream sector experiences the **largest profit swings**, thriving when commodity prices are high but facing significant challenges during price downturns. Margins can swing from year to year, and even quarter to quarter.

- This **asset-intensive industry** relies heavily on advanced technologies, including seismic imaging, unconventional drilling, and innovation, to enhance efficiency and reduce costs.

- **Cash flow** is highly sensitive to commodity price volatility, with high prices driving reinvestment into exploration, reserves development, and maintaining financial stability during downturns.

- Other key measures upstream oil and gas companies track include average realized price, lifting costs, reserve replacement ratio, and **employee safety measures** like total recordable incident rate or lost time injury frequency.

For current industry data, go to SellingtheBigPicture.com.

Compare your client's results to industry and S&P 500 results.

	Oil and Gas, Upstream Industry Avg.	S&P 500 Avg.
CASH		
Cash and Cash Equivalents as a % of Sales	16.2%	22.7%
Cash Generated from Operations as a % of Sales	46.3%	20.9%
PROFIT		
Gross Profit Margin %	51.4%	49.6%
Operating Profit Margin %	25.9%	23.2%
Net Profit Margin %	12.1%	12.9%
ASSETS		
Return on Assets (ROA) %	7.5%	8.4%
Equity Ratio	43.5%	33.7%
GROWTH		
Revenue Growth Rate %	10.2%	6.3%
Net Income Growth Rate %	23.8%	8.1%
PEOPLE		
Revenue per Employee	$0.8M	$1.6M

Notes:

- Because cash amounts can vary dramatically from company to company based on a company's overall "size," we've presented the numbers as a percentage of sales or revenue: the cash metric divided by total revenue or sales and then multiplied by 100.
- S&P 500 averages are calculated based on 3 years of annual reports as of July 2024, rounded. However, because certain financial industries, like asset management companies and diversified banks, hold large amounts of cash, they have been removed from the cash calculations.
- Most industry or sector averages are also calculated based on 3 years of annual reports from S&P 500 companies. However, certain companies or subsectors in the S&P sometimes skew the data far from what is typical for an industry, so we have occasionally removed some companies, subsectors, or periods from our calculations to provide a more accurate set of comparison data.

OIL AND GAS, MIDSTREAM

Highlights

- The midstream sector handles the gathering, processing, storing, and transporting of crude oil and natural gas, earning revenue through fee-based contracts that provide stable cash flow.

- Many midstream companies operate as master limited partnerships (MLPs), offering tax benefits and distributing a large portion of **cash flow** to investors.

- **Profits depend on operational efficiency** and throughput volume, supported by extensive pipeline networks, storage facilities, and processing infrastructure. **Revenue and profit growth** rates can vary significantly, based on demand shifts.

- While **cash flow is stable, significant reinvestment in infrastructure is required** to support demand growth and maintain capacity.

- Key metrics include throughput volume, pipeline utilization, and capital expenditures on infrastructure.

  For current industry data, go to SellingtheBigPicture.com.

Compare your client's results to industry and S&P 500 results.

	Oil and Gas, Midstream Industry Avg.	S&P 500 Avg.
CASH		
Cash and Cash Equivalents as a % of Sales	6.1%	22.7%
Cash Generated from Operations as a % of Sales	45.6%	20.9%
PROFIT		
Gross Profit Margin %	50.1%	49.6%
Operating Profit Margin %	27.5%	23.2%
Net Profit Margin %	13.3%	12.9%
ASSETS		
Return on Assets (ROA) %	3.17%	8.4%
Equity Ratio	34.9%	33.7%
GROWTH		
Revenue Growth Rate %	5.7%	6.3%
Net Income Growth Rate %	4.2%	8.1%
PEOPLE		
Revenue per Employee	$0.8M	$1.6M

Notes:

- Because cash amounts can vary dramatically from company to company based on a company's overall "size," we've presented the numbers as a percentage of sales or revenue: the cash metric divided by total revenue or sales and then multiplied by 100.
- S&P 500 averages are calculated based on 3 years of annual reports as of July 2024, rounded. However, because certain financial industries, like asset management companies and diversified banks, hold large amounts of cash, they have been removed from the cash calculations.
- Most industry or sector averages are also calculated based on 3 years of annual reports from S&P 500 companies. However, certain companies or subsectors in the S&P sometimes skew the data far from what is typical for an industry, so we have occasionally removed some companies, subsectors, or periods from our calculations to provide a more accurate set of comparison data.

OIL AND GAS, DOWNSTREAM

Highlights

- **Profits** depend on the crack spread, which is the difference between the cost of crude oil and the price of refined products. **Margins are generally thinner** than in the upstream or midstream segments.

- This **asset-intensive industry** relies on refining facilities, distribution networks, and retail operations, emphasizing efficiency and cost control to improve profitability.

- **Cash flow is steady but is reinvested** in maintenance, modernization, and compliance with environmental regulations and capital expenditures to upgrade facilities and improve efficiency.

- Key metrics include gross refining margin, refinery utilization rate, and **employee safety metrics** like total recordable incident rate.

For current industry data, go to SellingtheBigPicture.com.

Compare your client's results to industry and S&P 500 results.

	Oil and Gas, Downstream Industry Avg.	S&P 500 Avg.
CASH		
Cash and Cash Equivalents as a % of Sales	3.6%	22.7%
Cash Generated from Operations as a % of Sales	4.7%	20.9%
PROFIT		
Gross Profit Margin %	6.5%	49.6%
Operating Profit Margin %	3.1%	23.2%
Net Profit Margin %	2.5%	12.9%
ASSETS		
Return on Assets (ROA) %	5.2%	8.4%
Equity Ratio	37.1%	33.7%
GROWTH		
Revenue Growth Rate %	8.5%	6.3%
Net Income Growth Rate %	3.9%	8.1%
PEOPLE		
Revenue per Employee	$6.4M	$1.6M

Notes:

- Because cash amounts can vary dramatically from company to company based on a company's overall "size," we've presented the numbers as a percentage of sales or revenue: the cash metric divided by total revenue or sales and then multiplied by 100.

- S&P 500 averages are calculated based on 3 years of annual reports as of July 2024, rounded. However, because certain financial industries, like asset management companies and diversified banks, hold large amounts of cash, they have been removed from the cash calculations.

- Most industry or sector averages are also calculated based on 3 years of annual reports from S&P 500 companies. However, certain companies or subsectors in the S&P sometimes skew the data far from what is typical for an industry, so we have occasionally removed some companies, subsectors, or periods from our calculations to provide a more accurate set of comparison data.

PHARMACEUTICAL DEVELOPMENT AND MANUFACTURING

Highlights

- Because it takes ten or more years and roughly $2 billion to get a new drug to market, pharmaceutical companies need to ensure they have **high profit margins** to compensate for risk and **high levels of liquid assets** to fund ongoing innovation.

- Innovation in this industry isn't just about creating unique products but about creating **positive patient impact**. Accomplishing both allows them to charge premiums that drive **revenue growth** and **strong margins**.

- The primary **growth-driving asset** in this industry is a company's product pipeline.

- Two additional key measures these companies track due to their focus on innovation are R&D as a percentage of revenue (generally between 15% and 22%) and the vitality index (with a typical target of 25% to 50%), which is the percentage of revenue that comes from products launched in just the last few years.

For current industry data, go to SellingtheBigPicture.com.

Compare your client's results to industry and S&P 500 results.

	Pharma Devel. & Manufact. Industry Avg.	S&P 500 Avg.
CASH		
Cash and Cash Equivalents as a % of Sales	15.9%	22.7%
Cash Generated from Operations as a % of Sales	32.2%	20.9%
PROFIT		
Gross Profit Margin %	70.7%	49.6%
Operating Profit Margin %	28.9%	23.2%
Net Profit Margin %	21.9%	12.9%
ASSETS		
Return on Assets (ROA) %	10.6%	8.4%
Equity Ratio	30.3%	33.7%
GROWTH		
Revenue Growth Rate %	-0.3%	6.3%
Net Income Growth Rate %	-21.2%	8.1%
PEOPLE		
Revenue per Employee	$3.3M	$1.6M

Notes:

- Because cash amounts can vary dramatically from company to company based on a company's overall "size," we've presented the numbers as a percentage of sales or revenue: the cash metric divided by total revenue or sales and then multiplied by 100.
- S&P 500 averages are calculated based on 3 years of annual reports as of July 2024, rounded. However, because certain financial industries, like asset management companies and diversified banks, hold large amounts of cash, they have been removed from the cash calculations.
- Most industry or sector averages are also calculated based on 3 years of annual reports from S&P 500 companies. However, certain companies or subsectors in the S&P sometimes skew the data far from what is typical for an industry, so we have occasionally removed some companies, subsectors, or periods from our calculations to provide a more accurate set of comparison data.

REAL ESTATE DEVELOPMENT

Highlights

- Real estate or property developers build or redevelop properties, requiring **significant investment in assets** with high risk, which can influence their asset measures as they use debt to fund projects.

- They need **employees** with zoning expertise and strategic inventory management experience to help maintain profitability.

- The big pressures they can face, depending on economic and market conditions, are access to capital to fund land purchases and build out structures, supply chain hurdles, and cost inflation. Efficient sourcing of materials is critical to **profit**.

- Major developers in the industry also tend to be real estate investment trusts (REITs). Because they require large amounts of capital *and* REITs are required to distribute 90% of taxable income as dividends to **shareholders**, they need access to debt and equity markets, public and/or private. To generate profit and dividends, they focus on revenue optimization, cost management, and maintaining a healthy balance sheet. REITs regularly bring new properties online and sell existing properties, which can create a lot of volatility in earnings in any quarter or year. Traditional metrics aren't always helpful in assessing performance. Instead, they assess **profit** using net operating income, **cash** using adjusted funds from operations, and **assets** using net asset value, among other measures.

For current industry data, go to SellingtheBigPicture.com.

Compare your client's results to industry and S&P 500 results.

	Real Estate Development Industry Avg.	S&P 500 Avg.
CASH		
Cash and Cash Equivalents as a % of Sales	16.1%	22.7%
Cash Generated from Operations as a % of Sales	13.5%	20.9%
PROFIT		
Gross Profit Margin %	25.1%	49.6%
Operating Profit Margin %	18.7%	23.2%
Net Profit Margin %	14.8%	12.9%
ASSETS		
Return on Assets (ROA) %	17.5%	8.4%
Equity Ratio	58.5%	33.7%
GROWTH		
Revenue Growth Rate %	5.9%	6.3%
Net Income Growth Rate %	4.9%	8.1%
PEOPLE		
Revenue per Employee	$0.8M	$1.6M

Notes:

- Because cash amounts can vary dramatically from company to company based on a company's overall "size," we've presented the numbers as a percentage of sales or revenue: the cash metric divided by total revenue or sales and then multiplied by 100.
- S&P 500 averages are calculated based on 3 years of annual reports as of July 2024, rounded. However, because certain financial industries, like asset management companies and diversified banks, hold large amounts of cash, they have been removed from the cash calculations.
- Most industry or sector averages are also calculated based on 3 years of annual reports from S&P 500 companies. However, certain companies or subsectors in the S&P sometimes skew the data far from what is typical for an industry, so we have occasionally removed some companies, subsectors, or periods from our calculations to provide a more accurate set of comparison data.

RETAIL

Highlights

- Retail businesses are generally high volume, low margin, and capital-intensive businesses. They generate **significant cash flow**, and they generally have **small cash positions**.

- Because **profit margins are relatively small**, these businesses have a high level of inflation sensitivity. As input costs rise, profitability shrinks and the ability to invest in innovation slows.

- Retailers achieve small advantages over their peers through technology innovations such as supply chain optimization, in-store technology to **enhance the customer experience**, and e-commerce investments to **grow market share**.

- Retail companies track inventory turnover carefully (the more times, the better) to improve forecasting accuracy, operational and **business asset efficiency**, and strategy development and execution.

For current industry data, go to SellingtheBigPicture.com.

Compare your client's results to industry and S&P 500 results.

	Retail Industry Avg.	S&P 500 Avg.
CASH		
Cash and Cash Equivalents as a % of Sales	3.7%	22.7%
Cash Generated from Operations as a % of Sales	6.2%	20.9%
PROFIT		
Gross Profit Margin %	25.7%	49.6%
Operating Profit Margin %	7%	23.2%
Net Profit Margin %	4.7%	12.9%
ASSETS		
Return on Assets (ROA) %	8.6%	8.4%
Equity Ratio	30.2%	33.7%
GROWTH		
Revenue Growth Rate %	4.3%	6.3%
Net Income Growth Rate %	-4.9%	8.1%
PEOPLE		
Revenue per Employee	$10.3M	$1.6M

Notes:

- Because cash amounts can vary dramatically from company to company based on a company's overall "size," we've presented the numbers as a percentage of sales or revenue: the cash metric divided by total revenue or sales and then multiplied by 100.

- S&P 500 averages are calculated based on 3 years of annual reports as of July 2024, rounded. However, because certain financial industries, like asset management companies and diversified banks, hold large amounts of cash, they have been removed from the cash calculations.

- Most industry or sector averages are also calculated based on 3 years of annual reports from S&P 500 companies. However, certain companies or subsectors in the S&P sometimes skew the data far from what is typical for an industry, so we have occasionally removed some companies, subsectors, or periods from our calculations to provide a more accurate set of comparison data.

SEMICONDUCTOR MANUFACTURING

Highlights

- Because of **high profit margins**, companies in this space generate **strong cash flow from operations** and tend to have a lot of cash and cash equivalents.

- This industry can be cyclical, so **revenue and profit growth** rates can vary widely.

- Technology change is rapid, requiring companies to be close to **customer needs**, keep **innovative employees**, and often invest in **new assets**.

- Another key measure that companies in this industry track is R&D as a percentage of revenue, which usually falls between 10% and 12%.

For current industry data, go to SellingtheBigPicture.com.

Compare your client's results to industry and S&P 500 results.

	Semiconductor Industry Avg.	S&P 500 Avg.
CASH		
Cash and Cash Equivalents as a % of Sales	19.9%	22.7%
Cash Generated from Operations as a % of Sales	34.6%	20.9%
PROFIT		
Gross Profit Margin %	55%	49.6%
Operating Profit Margin %	30.2%	23.2%
Net Profit Margin %	24.1%	12.9%
ASSETS		
Return on Assets (ROA) %	16.6%	8.4%
Equity Ratio	53.8%	33.7%
GROWTH		
Revenue Growth Rate %	4.6%	6.3%
Net Income Growth Rate %	0.6%	8.1%
PEOPLE		
Revenue per Employee	$1.1M	$1.6M

Notes:

- Because cash amounts can vary dramatically from company to company based on a company's overall "size," we've presented the numbers as a percentage of sales or revenue: the cash metric divided by total revenue or sales and then multiplied by 100.
- S&P 500 averages are calculated based on 3 years of annual reports as of July 2024, rounded. However, because certain financial industries, like asset management companies and diversified banks, hold large amounts of cash, they have been removed from the cash calculations.
- Most industry or sector averages are also calculated based on 3 years of annual reports from S&P 500 companies. However, certain companies or subsectors in the S&P sometimes skew the data far from what is typical for an industry, so we have occasionally removed some companies, subsectors, or periods from our calculations to provide a more accurate set of comparison data.

SERVICES

Highlights

- Personal and professional service companies are **customer-centric** and labor intensive. They tend to offer various types of services to create diverse revenue streams. The industry tends to be fragmented, except for specialized services, which have a bigger barrier to entry and so tend to consolidate (think about the difference between a local plumbing company and a global corporate accounting firm like EY).

- **Profit margins vary widely** across the industry depending on the services offered.

- Companies providing specialty services tend to **invest significantly in their people**, including training and development and high salaries.

- Services companies are increasingly relying on subscriptions to improve the **customer experience**, lower the barrier to entry, and generate more **predictable cash flow**.

- Professional services companies track billable hours (time spent with particular customers) meticulously, and many also use earnings before interest, taxes, depreciation, and amortization (EBITDA) to analyze operational performance. Personal services companies track **customer satisfaction** metrics carefully.

For current industry data, go to SellingtheBigPicture.com.

Compare your client's results to industry and S&P 500 results.

	Services Industry Avg.	S&P 500 Avg.
CASH		
Cash and Cash Equivalents as a % of Sales	12.4%	22.7%
Cash Generated from Operations as a % of Sales	22.3%	20.9%
PROFIT		
Gross Profit Margin %	55.8%	49.6%
Operating Profit Margin %	25.8%	23.2%
Net Profit Margin %	19%	12.9%
ASSETS		
Return on Assets (ROA) %	14.9%	8.4%
Equity Ratio	43.8%	33.7%
GROWTH		
Revenue Growth Rate %	7.6%	6.3%
Net Income Growth Rate %	8.8%	8.1%
PEOPLE		
Revenue per Employee	$0.3M	$1.6M

Notes:

- Because cash amounts can vary dramatically from company to company based on a company's overall "size," we've presented the numbers as a percentage of sales or revenue: the cash metric divided by total revenue or sales and then multiplied by 100.
- S&P 500 averages are calculated based on 3 years of annual reports as of July 2024, rounded. However, because certain financial industries, like asset management companies and diversified banks, hold large amounts of cash, they have been removed from the cash calculations.
- Most industry or sector averages are also calculated based on 3 years of annual reports from S&P 500 companies. However, certain companies or subsectors in the S&P sometimes skew the data far from what is typical for an industry, so we have occasionally removed some companies, subsectors, or periods from our calculations to provide a more accurate set of comparison data.

SOFTWARE

Highlights

- The software industry is predominantly subscription (SaaS) or licensing based. This model leads to **strong, predictable cash flow**, particularly for mature firms with established customer bases. Startups may burn cash due to aggressive customer acquisition.

- This industry enjoys **high gross profit margins** (70% to 90%), as software incurs minimal costs once developed. Net margins vary depending on R&D and marketing spend.

- Companies rely on **minimal physical assets**. Rather, intellectual property, such as proprietary software and algorithms, along with cloud and data assets, form the bulk of the asset base, and investments are focused on funding R&D, sales, and marketing rather than fixed assets.

- Software companies serve diverse markets, from individual users (B2C) to enterprise solutions (B2B). Enterprise clients often account for the majority of revenue, but among all markets, reducing churn is critical and **customer retention** is a primary focus.

- Key metrics for the software industry include **annual recurring revenue** (ARR); net dollar retention (NDR), which tracks upsell success and customer retention; and R&D spend as a percentage of revenue, which measures focus on innovation and competitive advantage.

For current industry data, go to SellingtheBigPicture.com.

Compare your client's results to industry and S&P 500 results.

	Software Industry Avg.	S&P 500 Avg.
CASH		
Cash and Cash Equivalents as a % of Sales	42.7%	22.7%
Cash Generated from Operations as a % of Sales	36.9%	20.9%
PROFIT		
Gross Profit Margin %	76.2%	49.6%
Operating Profit Margin %	22.4%	23.2%
Net Profit Margin %	16.4%	12.9%
ASSETS		
Return on Assets (ROA) %	9.4%	8.4%
Equity Ratio	12.2%	33.7%
GROWTH		
Revenue Growth Rate %	10%	6.3%
Net Income Growth Rate %	19.4%	8.1%
PEOPLE		
Revenue per Employee	$1.2M	$1.6M

Notes:

- Because cash amounts can vary dramatically from company to company based on a company's overall "size," we've presented the numbers as a percentage of sales or revenue: the cash metric divided by total revenue or sales and then multiplied by 100.
- S&P 500 averages are calculated based on 3 years of annual reports as of July 2024, rounded. However, because certain financial industries, like asset management companies and diversified banks, hold large amounts of cash, they have been removed from the cash calculations.
- Most industry or sector averages are also calculated based on 3 years of annual reports from S&P 500 companies. However, certain companies or subsectors in the S&P sometimes skew the data far from what is typical for an industry, so we have occasionally removed some companies, subsectors, or periods from our calculations to provide a more accurate set of comparison data.

TELECOMMUNICATIONS

Highlights

- Telecommunications is a competitive business with a few major players competing to keep and steal subscribers (**customers**) from each other. This tends to **drive down profit margins**, which are typically lower than other industries.

- Companies in this industry are **asset intensive** as they must invest heavily in building and maintaining networks. Network speed and reliability are critical to attracting and keeping customers.

- Competition keeps **organic growth rates lower**, making acquisitions of other companies a common strategy.

- Additional key measures important in this industry are average revenue per user (ARPU), which is around $31 per month, and net subscriber additions, which tracks the number of new subscribers gained minus the number of subscribers lost.

For current industry data, go to SellingtheBigPicture.com.

Compare your client's results to industry and S&P 500 results.

	Telecom Industry Avg.	S&P 500 Avg.
CASH		
Cash and Cash Equivalents as a % of Sales	6.3%	22.7%
Cash Generated from Operations as a % of Sales	25.7%	20.9%
PROFIT		
Gross Profit Margin %	48.1%	49.6%
Operating Profit Margin %	32.2%	23.2%
Net Profit Margin %	10.7%	12.9%
ASSETS		
Return on Assets (ROA) %	4%	8.4%
Equity Ratio	27.5%	33.7%
GROWTH		
Revenue Growth Rate %	-1.5%	6.3%
Net Income Growth Rate %	2.5%	8.1%
PEOPLE		
Revenue per Employee	$6.1M	$1.6M

Notes:

- Because cash amounts can vary dramatically from company to company based on a company's overall "size," we've presented the numbers as a percentage of sales or revenue: the cash metric divided by total revenue or sales and then multiplied by 100.
- S&P 500 averages are calculated based on 3 years of annual reports as of July 2024, rounded. However, because certain financial industries, like asset management companies and diversified banks, hold large amounts of cash, they have been removed from the cash calculations.
- Most industry or sector averages are also calculated based on 3 years of annual reports from S&P 500 companies. However, certain companies or subsectors in the S&P sometimes skew the data far from what is typical for an industry, so we have occasionally removed some companies, subsectors, or periods from our calculations to provide a more accurate set of comparison data.

UTILITIES SECTOR

Highlights

- The utilities sector includes regulated electric, gas, and water companies; independent power producers; and renewable energy companies.

- Due to the essential nature of utilities services, they are typically heavily regulated to ensure fair pricing, reliability, and accessibility for all. In some cases, these companies may even be government-owned. As a result, **profit margins** are typically modest.

- Utilities rely on **significant assets**, leading to high interest expenses, depreciation of long-term assets, and ongoing infrastructure maintenance, all of which contribute to constrained profitability.

- Utilities typically benefit from **predictable cash flows**, which can be reinvested into the business **to support operations and growth**.

- Environmental, social, and governance (ESG) considerations in the utilities industry are driven by both consumer demand for sustainability and an opportunity to **increase profit margins**. Renewable energy companies, for example, often achieve higher margins because their operations are less resource-intensive once infrastructure is established. For instance, while installing solar panels on the roof of your home involves a significant upfront cost, the maintenance expenses over time are minimal.

For current industry data, go to SellingtheBigPicture.com.

Compare your client's results to industry and S&P 500 results.

	Utilities Sector Avg.	S&P 500 Avg.
CASH		
Cash and Cash Equivalents as a % of Sales	5.8%	22.7%
Cash Generated from Operations as a % of Sales	18.1%	20.9%
PROFIT		
Gross Profit Margin %	40.7%	49.6%
Operating Profit Margin %	29.5%	23.2%
Net Profit Margin %	10.0%	12.9%
ASSETS		
Return on Assets (ROA) %	2.2%	8.4%
Equity Ratio	27.4%	33.7%
GROWTH		
Revenue Growth Rate %	3.8%	6.3%
Net Income Growth Rate %	17.7%	8.1%
PEOPLE		
Revenue per Employee	$0.7M	$1.6M

Notes:
- Because cash amounts can vary dramatically from company to company based on a company's overall "size," we've presented the numbers as a percentage of sales or revenue: the cash metric divided by total revenue or sales and then multiplied by 100.
- S&P 500 averages are calculated based on 3 years of annual reports as of July 2024, rounded. However, because certain financial industries, like asset management companies and diversified banks, hold large amounts of cash, they have been removed from the cash calculations.
- Most industry or sector averages are also calculated based on 3 years of annual reports from S&P 500 companies. However, certain companies or subsectors in the S&P sometimes skew the data far from what is typical for an industry, so we have occasionally removed some companies, subsectors, or periods from our calculations to provide a more accurate set of comparison data.

WASTE DISPOSAL

Highlights

- Waste disposal companies earn revenue from waste collection, disposal services, and increasingly, recycling and waste-to-energy (WTE) programs. Contracts with local governments, industrial clients, and commercial businesses often drive long-term revenue streams.

- While the steady demand for waste management leads to **stable cash flow, profit margins** vary depending on service type (higher for hazardous waste, lower for residential collection) and geographic reach. Recycling operations often have tighter margins due to fluctuating commodity prices.

- Waste disposal requires **significant investments in assets**—equipment, maintenance, and landfill development and management.

- The industry relies on **a large base of employees**, including drivers, equipment operators, and landfill workers. Labor shortages and wage inflation can impact profitability.

- Key metrics include tons of waste processed, percentage of waste diverted into recycling programs, fleet efficiency, and landfill utilization rate (a measure of remaining landfill lifespan, critical for long-term planning).

For current industry data, go to SellingtheBigPicture.com.

Compare your client's results to industry and S&P 500 results.

	Waste Disposal Industry Avg.	S&P 500 Avg.
CASH		
Cash and Cash Equivalents as a % of Sales	0.5%	22.7%
Cash Generated from Operations as a % of Sales	24.4%	20.9%
PROFIT		
Gross Profit Margin %	39.2%	49.6%
Operating Profit Margin %	28.7%	23.2%
Net Profit Margin %	10.8%	12.9%
ASSETS		
Return on Assets (ROA) %	5.8%	8.4%
Equity Ratio	30.2%	33.7%
GROWTH		
Revenue Growth Rate %	7.1%	6.3%
Net Income Growth Rate %	9.3%	8.1%
PEOPLE		
Revenue per Employee	$0.8M	$1.6M

Notes:

- Because cash amounts can vary dramatically from company to company based on a company's overall "size," we've presented the numbers as a percentage of sales or revenue: the cash metric divided by total revenue or sales and then multiplied by 100.
- S&P 500 averages are calculated based on 3 years of annual reports as of July 2024, rounded. However, because certain financial industries, like asset management companies and diversified banks, hold large amounts of cash, they have been removed from the cash calculations.
- Most industry or sector averages are also calculated based on 3 years of annual reports from S&P 500 companies. However, certain companies or subsectors in the S&P sometimes skew the data far from what is typical for an industry, so we have occasionally removed some companies, subsectors, or periods from our calculations to provide a more accurate set of comparison data.

More Resources

Now that you've read the book on leveraging business acumen in your sales approach, it's time to walk the talk. Continue your learning and expand your success by going to

SellingtheBigPicture.com

To help you succeed in your next client conversation, you can download, watch, or review a host of free resources.

» Client alignment and value proposition workbook (Resource 1)

» Navigating the Financials worksheet

» Industry data and insights

» Financial statements interrelationships one-sheet

» ROI 101

» IFRS accounting principles one-sheet for international company analysis

» Business acumen glossary

And we're adding more helpful tools and insights to our website all the time, so be sure to check back often.

Notes

1 Forrester, "Why Buyers Don't Want to Meet with Your Salespeople," September 29, 2014, available at www.forrester.com/blogs/14-09-29-why_dont_buyers_want_to_meet_with_your_salespeople/.

2 "The LinkedIn State of Sales Report 2020: Global Edition," p. 14, available at business.linkedin.com/content/dam/me/business/en-us/sales-solutions/resources/pdfs/state-of-sales-global-edition-2020-r5.pdf.

3 Mark Wayshak, "23 Surprising New Sales Statistics for 2023 from Our Groundbreaking Studies!" Sales Insights Lab, available at salesinsightslab.com/sales-research/.

4 Nick McGarth, "David Mitchell: Me & My Money" [interview], *The Daily Mail*, July 16, 2008, available at www.thisismoney.co.uk/money/meandmymoney/article-1637165/David-Mitchell-Me--money.html.

5 Lawrence Cunningham, *The Essays of Warren Buffett*, 8th ed. (Cunningham Group, 2023), 318.

6 Tim Cook, Apple Inc. Q2 2024 Earnings Call [transcript], May 2, 2024, available at finance.yahoo.com/news/apple-inc-nasdaq-aapl-q2-162038149.html

7 Jim Collins, *Built to Last* (HarperBusiness, 2002), 55.

8 UPS Inc., "UPS Releases 1Q 2023 Earnings," available at investors.ups.com/news-events/press-releases/detail/2090/ups-releases-1q-2023-earnings

9 Cathy Booth, "Steve's Job: Restart Apple," *Time*, August 18, 1997, available at https://time.com/archive/6731292/steves-job-restart-apple/

10 Jason Aten, "Delta CEO Ed Bastian Finally Responds to the Airline's Controversy: 'We Probably Went Too Far,'" Inc.com, September 27, 2023, available at www.inc.com/jason-aten/deltas-ceo-ed-bastian-finally-responded-to-airlines-skymiles-controversy-we-probably-went-too-far.html.

11 "Gallup, State of the Global Workplace: 2024 Report, 3," available at www.gallup.com/workplace/349484/state-of-the-global-workplace.aspx.

12 DDI, "Fragile Workforces Keep CEOs Up at Night," Global Leadership Forecast 2023, available at www.ddiworld.com/global-leadership-forecast-2023/ceo-challenges.

13 Mike Sievert, "T-Mobile US First Quarter 2020 Earnings Call," May 6, 2020; transcript available at s29.q4cdn.com/310188824/files/doc_financials/2020/q1/TMUS-USQ_Transcript_2020_Q1.pdf.

14 Tim Koller, James Manyika, and Sree Ramaswamy, "The Case Against Corporate Short Termism," *Milken Institute Review*, August 4, 2017, available at www.milkenreview.org/articles/the-case-against-corporate-short-termism.

15 Dale Carnegie, *How to Win Friends and Influence People*, rev. ed. (Simon & Schuster, 2022), 99.

Acknowledgments

WE COULD NOT HAVE WRITTEN A BOOK we're so proud of without the support of an incredible team of people who made significant contributions throughout the process.

To our colleagues at Acumen Learning—those who lead and shape the culture, impact, and influence we have together—you are a vital part of this book. You make coming to work a joy and truly embody our company vision: "Work is a big part of life, and we believe it should be meaningful!" You've certainly brought that meaning to us.

A heartfelt thank you to our assistant and business manager, Sharon Biegler, who has been with us from the very beginning. She keeps everything running smoothly.

To Brent Barclay, our COO and culture champion—what a powerful combination.

To Mike Wright, not only a gifted writer and contributor to this book, but also a talented sales and marketing director.

To Kenny Snarr and Greg Kendare, whose insights—including those shared for this book—are consistently valuable.

To Stephen M.R. Covey, a remarkable thinker, leader, and mentor.

And to our talented editor, Lari Bishop—thank you for your expertise and care in shaping this book.

This project—from its core concepts to its insights for salespeople—reflects the contributions of many talented friends at Acumen Learning, including: Kelvin Brents, Steve Call, Rebecca Cooper, Isabella Cope, David Covey, Stephen Covey, Cam Crockett, Ryan Hunt, Bailee Marsh, Monty Magleby, Andrew Mendenhall, Haley Ollerton,

Brooklyn Parks, Brian Peterson, Julie Rasmussen, Ron Saffell, Lisa Stirland, Curtis Warren, and Weston Winegar. This team does an extraordinary amount of critical work for our clients day in and day out, and we are honored to work alongside them.

We've also learned so much from our clients, whose experiences helped shape this book. While bad business behavior often makes the headlines, we've had the privilege of working with organizations and leaders doing meaningful, inspiring work. We're proud to have partnered with 34 Fortune 50 companies and many others, collaborating with exceptional people who just so happen to work in business. To our clients: We learn from you every day, and we hope you gain as much from us as we do from you

Special Thanks from Kevin

Over the years, I've been fortunate to work alongside many brilliant colleagues who have offered invaluable advice and unwavering support. None more so than my co-author, Ben Cook—a truly exceptional business partner and friend.

I am deeply grateful to my wonderful parents, Lloyd and Kathleen Cope, whose encouragement has never wavered. My mom continues to support me in this life, and my dad, from the next, still inspires me every day.

Most importantly, I thank my wife, Karen, and our children—Austin and his wife, Brittany; Spencer and his wife, Meghan; Ryan and his wife, Michelle; Conner; Isabella; and Noelle—as well as my eight beloved grandchildren. You are my greatest joy, and I feel truly blessed to share this grand adventure of life with you.

Special Thanks from Ben

This journey through life and career has been a beautiful and, at times, serendipitous one. At every step, I could not have had the necessary courage or motivation without the support and partnership of my wife, Michelle, who is my truest example of goodness and strength. Along with Michelle, the heart of my life are our four children—Bailee, Noah, Olivia, and Lily. I also had the greatest of influences and guides from early on by having two of the best brothers a guy could ever hope for: Brad and Cory Cook.

Along with those in my family, I have been fortunate to have as advisors, examples, friends, and confidants—for decades since our time in Austin—Greg Kandare, Jon Pollock, Scott Hardy, Joe Dallimore, Steve Coleman, and Rob Sorensen.

Thank you all for the impact you have had on who I am and who I strive to become.

About the Authors

Kevin Cope is the author of the #1 *Wall Street Journal* and *New York Times* bestseller, *Seeing the Big Picture*. His passion for helping people understand how they can make a difference in their companies has made him a successful executive, a trusted resource and confidant to business leaders from around the world, and a sought-after keynote speaker. For over 30 years, Kevin has promoted the idea that the brightest minds in business—no matter their role and no matter their experience—understand the essence of how a company makes money through the 5 Business Drivers, and they use this knowledge to make good things happen for the company. In other words, they have strong business acumen.

Kevin is the founder and CEO of Acumen Learning, a training and development company that has gone on to teach Kevin's ideas and business models to some of the world's most respected and successful organizations, including many of the Fortune 50—Cigna, General Motors, Humana, Lockheed Martin, T-Mobile, Verizon, Walmart, and many, many others. He helps teams of businesspeople understand how to set and achieve goals that ensure the long-term, sustainable profitability of their company while supporting its mission.

Ben Cook has a talent for engaging people at all levels within teams, from rising managers to global corporate executives. His early experiences as a teacher, then an MBA that offered a range of experience in corporate leadership roles with Fortune 50 companies, and his years spent living abroad in Greece, Saudi Arabia, and Argentina have given him deep insights into how to help teams across organizations align on the fundamentals of success.

As president of Acumen Learning, Ben leverages his product-line finance, strategy, global brand management, and sales leadership experience to offer value to clients. He leads development of Acumen Learning's customized curriculum and client work for global companies like GE HealthCare and Johnson & Johnson, and works directly with teams from Apple, JP Morgan, KPMG, Medtronic, Novartis, Philips, Canon, Dell, and many more companies.

About Acumen Learning

Your sales teams need business acumen training.

If salespeople don't know how their clients make money (and research suggests that most don't), how can they reach executives or create compelling value propositions? They can't! Not understanding business is costing you business.

New York Times bestselling author Kevin Cope founded the world's leading business acumen training organization, Acumen Learning, to teach professionals about the business of their own businesses *and* their customers' businesses. Since 2002, more than 500,000 professionals in more than 35 countries and 34 of the Fortune 50 have counted on Acumen Learning to drive their business results.

What is a lack of business acumen on your team costing you?

Can every leader or team member in your company explain your company's money-making process? And can they do it in such a way that helps them connect it to your strategy and priorities or engage employees? If not, you're losing money. How many decisions are made too quickly or not quickly enough? How many of your team members don't understand what your CEO talked about in the last earnings call?

Let's transform your organization today!

To receive more information on learning these skills or becoming a trainer for your organization, call 877-224-5444 or go to

www.AcumenLearning.com